T0194810

Other works by Enoch Elijah:

Insights for Believers
God Is

A Frayed World

Prepares for Harvest

ENOCH ELIJAH

WESTBOW
PRESS®
A DIVISION OF THOMAS NELSON
& ZONDERVAN

This book is a work of non-fiction. Unless otherwise noted, the author and the publisher make no explicit guarantees as to the accuracy of the information contained in this book and in some cases, names of people and places have been altered to protect their privacy.

WestBow Press books may be ordered through booksellers or by contacting:

WestBow Press
A Division of Thomas Nelson & Zondervan
1663 Liberty Drive
Bloomington, IN 47403
www.westbowpress.com
844-714-3454

Scripture taken from the King James Version of the Bible.

ISBN: 978-1-6642-5928-7 (sc)
ISBN: 978-1-6642-5927-0 (hc)
ISBN: 978-1-6642-5926-3 (e)

Library of Congress Control Number: 2022903703

Print information available on the last page.

WestBow Press rev. date: 03/22/2022

DEDICATION

This know also, that in the last days perilous times shall come.

(2 Timothy 3:1)

This work is for those who have had thoughts about the last days and what they mean for us alive during these times.

EPIGRAPH

The number two can illustrate division or differences. The differences can be of evil or be of good. The difference between good and evil reveals the dissimilarities between them.

This same principle is found between rivals in the Bible such as Cain and Abel, Hagar and Sarah, Ishmael and Isaac, Esau and Jacob, David and Saul. There are also disparities within the personalities of individuals such as Jacob/Israel, Simon Peter, and Saul/Paul.

2022 will be a time of division and differences resulting in conflict externally with the world and internally within each of us.

We can only assess differences during these times through the witness of Jesus Christ through prophecy. The revelation of Christ will help us gain understanding through divine inspiration by the Spirit of God.

Then we will know our purpose in the fullness of Jesus Christ our Lord in these last days. Overcoming divisions and differences caused by distinctions between good and evil; right and wrong; truth and deception.

> *The Lord bless thee, and keep thee:*
>
> *The Lord make his face shine upon thee, and be gracious unto thee:*
>
> *The Lord lift up his countenance upon thee, and give thee peace.*
>
> *(Numbers 6:24-26)*

CONTENTS

PREFACE

This book will discuss the current social pressures and it will give detail of how to overcome the internal struggles that are becoming rampant throughout society. It illustrates characteristics between the people of Israel and Christ's Disciples to assist the spiritual linkage between the two groups being presented in scripture.

The Israeli people were in bondage to Nebuchadnezzar due to their refusal to stop serving Baal a pagan god. They practiced rituals of worship, offering of children as sacrifices, and witchcraft (2 Kings 17:7-17). The Body of Christ is also struggling to take a stand against the worldly practices of today.

How do we overcome today's struggles? The imagery in the book of Zechariah illustrates the capability of the true and wise God to provide outcomes for Israel and the Body of Christ.

The Prophet Zechariah was to provide spiritual testimony to encourage the rebuilding of the temple as the people returned from the Babylonian captivity (Jeremiah 29:10). This is also the goal of this work to give testimony that inspires a closer walk with God as we become the living temples of God.

In our walk the characteristics relating to the name used when referring to God is important. It helps our spiritual realization of who He is. When I refer to God, by using all capitalized letters in the word LORD (Adonay – Old Testament); this is a reference of Him as the eternal all powerful LORD (God of all gods). At times I will also use the word God (Theos – New Testament) to mention Him as the God of the universe and creation.

INTRODUCTION

A FRAYED WORLD!

We are living in a time of constant change. Life as it was five years ago has disappeared.

There are many factions competing for the control of our existence. Society is restructuring how we interact, our thoughts relating to equality, and justice. Making identification of those who are different in appearance, thought, and belief a simple task.

This restructuring is causing individual convictions to be ignored. To force individuals to line up with the new society. The direction society is moving aligns with Babylon the great, the mother of harlots and abominations of the earth.

Humanity is emphasizing our social development has outgrown the Bible and the LORD God. This type of independent thought dates back to the "Garden of Eden" and is shown repeatedly in the Bible.

Look at these two scriptures relating to Babylon:

> *I saw a woman sit upon a scarlet coloured beast, full of names of blasphemy, having seven heads and ten horns.*
>
> *(Revelation 17:3)*

And upon her forehead was a name written, Mystery, Babylon the great, the mother of harlots and abominations of the earth.

(Revelation 17:5)

The idolatrous thinking of Babylon is plaguing the world. The same pagan activities that Israel practiced that sent them into bondage are present in our country and the rest of the world. Babylonian captivity and the mystery of its spiritual importance will be discussed as we review the events in the book of Zachariah.

At the timing of the return of Israel from Babylon the LORD spoke to Zechariah saying:

Therefore say thou unto them, Thus saith the LORD of hosts; Turn ye unto me, saith the LORD of hosts, and I will turn unto you, saith the LORD of hosts.

(Zechariah 1:3)

And I am very sore displeased with the heathen that are at ease: for I was but a little displeased, and they helped forward the affliction.

Therefore thus saith the LORD; I am returned to Jerusalem with mercies: my house shall be built in it saith the LORD of hosts, and a line shall be stretched forth upon Jerusalem.

(Zechariah 1:14-15)

The LORD is calling humanity to return unto Him. In the Epigraph I mentioned external and internal division and differences. The scripture above illudes to their impact due to the worldly influence of society. Yet, the LORD is measuring the outcomes of what is thought to be social progress.

The world becomes at ease and secure being confident the mischief they have propagated will cause the adversity needed to suppress belief in the LORD.

When the people of the LORD are not in their place due to complacency or because of distraction it allows the world to be at ease being able to move forward without confrontation.

We must turn to the LORD; to enable Him to turn to us and be our shield in times of adversity.

> *The* LORD *shewed me four carpenters.*
>
> *Then said I, what come these to do? And he spake, saying, These are the horns which have scattered Judah, so that no man did lift up his head: but these are come (the carpenters) to fray them, to cast out the horns of the Gentiles, which lifted up their horn over the land of Judah to scatter it.*
>
> *(Zechariah 1:20-21)*

The word fray[1] means to shudder with terror, to fear, be afraid, and discomfited. The word Judah means praise unto the LORD.

The LORD of hosts is ready to lead us in these last days as He frays the horns of the wicked. The horn's goal is to scatter those who give praise unto the LORD of hosts preventing the work of salvation from occurring.

The divisions and differences are all about the harvest of souls. Our victory is not saving the current world structure. It is about saving souls from the deception of this world structure.

Humanity stands frayed as the differences between the thoughts of society and Believers begin to be self-evident. The

Word of God being shared through His people encouraging others to accept His call is the mission.

> *For we are his workmanship, created in Christ Jesus unto good works, which God hath before ordained that we should walk in them.*
>
> *(Ephesians 2:10)*

When we are called into the family of God; we become the workmanship of the master carpenter and builder of all (John 1:3).

> *Wherefore lay apart all filthiness* (things that make filthy*) and superfluity* (superabundance*) of naughtiness* (evil mindset*), and receive with meekness the engrafted* (implanted*) word, which is able to save your souls.*
>
> *But be ye doers of the word, and not hearers only, deceiving your own selves.*
>
> *(James 1:21-22)*

This scripture was written by the son of Mary and Joseph, the half-brother of our Lord (Matthew 13:55). He is advising us to walk in our call being doers of the Word.

The prophets Haggai and Zechariah delivered messages unto the people of Israel to encourage them along the way as they reestablished the temple.

> *Then spake Haggai the Lord's messenger in the Lord's message unto the people, saying, I am with you, saith the Lord.*
>
> *(Haggai 1:13)*

The word message in this verse denotes a dispatch from God issued through a prophet, priest, or teacher (Strong's Exhaustive Concordance).

Each chapter in this book will dispatch a message intended to inspire and enlighten the reader on what the Spirit of God is doing in these last days.

Fear not the LORD is with His people!

KEY THOUGHTS PAGE

Weakened Beliefs

The deterioration of the internal belief system of many is occurring.

I want to share some background about the origin of the influences we experience today that is causing this deterioration.

The Babylonian kingdom started with Nim'rod (Genesis 10:10). His kingdom began with Babel, one of four cities he founded in the land of Shinar (Iraq).

Babylon is representative of the confusion in the world that occurred at the tower of Babel. It was due to the desire of the people to build a city and a tower reaching into the gates of heaven (Genesis 11:4-9).

They wanted to make a name for themselves distinguishing their independence and control to hinder any other events that would scatter them on earth. This was during the time after the flood (Genesis 8:14) when there were events that happened out of the control of humans.

> *And he cried mightily with a strong voice, saying,*
> *Babylon the great is fallen, is fallen, and is become*

the habitation of devils, and the hold of every foul spirit, and the cage of every unclean bird.

For all nations have drunk of the wine of the wrath of her fornication, and the kings of the earth have committed fornication with her, and the merchants of the earth are waxed rich through the abundance of her delicacies.

And I heard another voice from heaven, saying, Come out of her, my people, that ye be not partakers of her sins, and that ye receive not of her plagues.

(Revelation 18:2-4)

Is it a coincidence that the city that started rebellion after the flood is the same empire that placed Israel in bondage? These same philosophies are causing the divisions in the world today.

Deception is an important tool of the world system to create division. It causes the world to be fractured and torn resulting in the appearance of the man of sin.

World norms today are self-reliance, devaluing God's Word, and dependence on science and technology to guide us are part of this deception. These are mentalities driving the thought that an unseen God is useless. How we use innovation becomes the issue.

The following paragraphs will discuss behavioral attributes which would influence many to answer unfavorably about the existence or the need for God. Individual characteristics of each person are developed by their beliefs, and the evidence is demonstrated through their behaviors.

Your belief system is what governs your reality!

Society is shaping the beliefs of individuals through the news, internet, and social media. If you hear it multiple times, it must be true. This is a huge deception! Self-indulgence is being demonstrated in the belief that person's individual rights are more important than anything else.

The narrative of society is for Christianity to practice the greatest commandment, the commandment of love in every situation. The narrative stresses an outcome for Christians to overlook biblical teachings that disagree with the new norms. If biblical teachings are not overlooked, then Christians are labeled prejudice and intolerant.

The Bible is the standard for life's values and truth.

> *Knowing this, that the law is not made for a righteous man, but for the lawless and disobedient, for the ungodly and for sinners, for unholy and profane, for murderers of fathers and murderers of mothers, for manslayers,*
>
> *For whoremongers, for them that defile themselves with mankind, for menstealers, for liars, for perjured persons, and if there be any other thing that is contrary to sound doctrine;*
>
> *(1 Timothy 1:9-10)*

Paul has accurately summed it up; all these things are what destroys society! We have a court system with laws to punish those who break them. So why is the Bible such a prejudice unfair document? The menstealers are the one's propagating this lie.

What is a menstealer[2]? It is the combination of the Greek word ekeph from the word akaph. Akaph means to curve as with a burden, to urge a craving. The word ekeph means a load implying a stroke to others dignity.

Menstealers burden and load others with urgings that cause them to curve (turn), crave, and embrace ideas that strike a blow to the core of their dignity. Causing them to be stolen away from belief in basic doctrines of the Bible.

They corrupt the thinking of others as they are weakening the belief system in the LORD and Jesus Christ.

> *And then shall many be offended, and shall betray*
> *one another, and shall hate one another.*
>
> *(Matthew 24:10)*

As Jesus prophesied the people in the world will become easily offended, causing some to stumble because of betrayal and hatred of one another. Cancel culture is a technique of menstealers. They are the ones who are prejudice and intolerant.

Menstealers believe Christians should practice the commandment of love in every situation. Ignoring the reason, the LORD gave the commandments.

The word commandments[3] means to give an authoritative *prescription of precepts,* that if followed, bring blessings of a full life. The commandments are not to restrict us; they are to guide us to a full life.

Are we guided to a full life by giving a person everything they want and agreeing with everything they do? Is this a demonstration of love?

Does a parent hate their child because they correct them when they display behavior not beneficial to leading a successful life?

> *He that spareth his rod hateth his son: but he that*
> *loveth him chasteneth him betimes.*
>
> *(Proverbs 13:24)*

Parents love their children; therefore, they correct them. Love desires the best for others. God's best provided the ability to secure eternal life through our choice to believe in Jesus Christ.

There is an increasing focus to develop a culture that removes the ability of choice to believe what the Bible says. Forcing acceptance of the social norms. God does not even force us to choose Him!

The culture of tolerance is causing separation from God. It leads to the concept that truth is what each person thinks is right for them.

> Woe unto them that call evil good, and good evil; that put darkness for light, and light for darkness; that put bitter for sweet, and sweet for bitter!
>
> Woe unto them that are wise in their own eyes, and prudent in their own sight!
>
> Woe unto them that are mighty to drink wine, and men of strength to mingle strong drink:
>
> Which justify the wicked for reward, and take away the righteousness of the righteous from him!
>
> (Isaiah 5:20-23)

The culture described in these verses is what we are witnessing today. People who are wise in their own eyes. They call good being evil and evil being good for the purpose of self-indulgence.

They justify the wicked and attempt to take away righteousness from the people of God, by labeling them as prejudice or intolerant for the benefit of those who practice unrighteousness.

> For men shall be lovers of their own selves, covetous, boasters, proud, blasphemers, disobedient to parents, unthankful, unholy,

Without natural affection, trucebreakers, false accusers, incontinent, fierce, despisers of those that are good,

(2 Timothy 3:2-3)

When people follow beliefs and doctrines influenced by unrighteousness and then speak evil of anyone that disagrees, they become blasphemers[4]. They vilify or speak evil of the truth. This is what's causing society to become frayed and torn.

Even the Body of Christ is beginning to see divisions and debate on whether the original intent of scripture is suitable for today. I wonder at times if the fear of offending others is causing a willingness to tolerate what's happening, or is it something worse!

So the servants of the householder came and said unto him, Sir, didst not thou sow good seed in thy field? From whence then hath it tares?

He said unto them, An enemy hath done this. The servants said unto him, Wilt thou then that we go and gather them up?

But he said, Nay: lest while ye gather up the tares, ye root up also the wheat with them.

(Matthew 13:27-29)

Tares[5] resemble wheat in appearance except the seeds are black. The seeds are poisonous to people causing sleepiness, nausea, convulsions, and even death. They appear to be wheat but are a destructive imposter.

As mentioned in Amos 8:14 the people of today swear[6] oaths by repeating false philosophies affirming unrighteous practices. By doing this, they embrace those practices.

Our young women and men are fainting for thirst (Amos 8:13) for lack of the Word of God that can clearly distinguish truth from lies. The phrase virgins and young[7] men are not speaking about children. This references women and men of full age and strength (young adults) starting their quest into life.

The young women and men in our nation are challenged with policies and opinions taught in our educational system that will strike at the core of their belief system. Education is only education when it inspires reflection to create higher levels of understanding. Sharing of a specific world view for the purpose of indoctrination is not education.

The deceit occurring is impacting thoughts and practices within the Church as well, causing confusion of what to think or believe. The famine of the Word, caused by worldly thinking and practices, can be extinguished in each of our lives. We just need to stand on the Word and maintain the free moral agency God created.

Especially, as we evolve and expand our natural knowledge at a faster rate than ever before. The fixation around technology is becoming addictive.

This fixation is dangerous. The meaning of words is changing based on the current social mindset. Because of this fixation the original purpose and meaning of documents must be changed, including the Bible and our US Constitution. The request for change will allow official papers to become living documents flexing with the changes in public opinion.

You can see the results of technology and science in Revelation 13:15. I believe this image is a result of technological advances. Specifically, the ability to give what seems to be rational thought and understanding to computer components and hardware, leading to virtual interaction.

As technology advances, I believe the LORD has started the

beginning of the birth pains (sorrows), to translate this current world into the Kingdom of His dear Son.

The changes in culture and the belief system of mankind will require us to have faith in God more than ever. No, it will require the faith of God to operate in our daily lives.

Disorder, distress, disaster, and uncertainty are signs of the end times. Remember God is the ultimate reality. Seek Him and He can give you peace. Speak to your children, family, and friends so that they will not faint in the coming years.

World leaders call what is happening the "Great Reset". Reset of what? They are redefining what is essential for the defense of mankind (Nimrod's Babylonian thought process).

Will God be essential? Will a person's status authorize them to make unilateral recommendations for society? Will all be required to conform as monetary, communication, and government systems implement policies creating more control over our lives?

Why doesn't the LORD intervene to stop a system that puts people in bondage? I believe this is the only way He can show all mankind the difference between His rule and the rule of satan. This is the process for the Lord Jesus to create for Himself a bride that is true.

If the LORD intervened, He would basically eliminate our free will. The spirit of Babylon is intervening to force all to comply to its beliefs. Intervention by the LORD would create an environment of influence that persuades people to accept Him not out of love, but out of necessity. A choice made from necessity would not pass the test for sustainability throughout eternity.

The development of our belief system in Christ, as we work through challenges and trials is what passes the test for entrance into eternity.

KEY THOUGHTS PAGE

Leave Babylon

There is a life and death decision everyone must make. I'm not speaking of death for the body; I'm talking about eternal life or eternal separation from the LORD (death).

> *And Elijah came unto all the people, and said, How long halt ye between two opinions? If the LORD be God, follow him: but if Baal, then follow him. And the people answered him not a word.*
>
> *(1Kings 18:21)*

Baal worship is at the center of the Babylonian influence. We must decide who we will serve.

> *Deliver thyself, O Zion, that dwellest with the daughter of Babylon.*
>
> *(Zechariah 2:7)*

The LORD is calling us to deliver ourselves from the world (leave spiritual Babylon). Malat is the Hebrew word for deliver[8] to escape, slip away, release, rescue.

This call for deliverance is also meant for all people. Escaping the world to be born into the Kingdom of the LORD. This is an exciting time as the Body of Christ takes its place.

> *Then he answered and spake unto me, saying, This is the word of the LORD unto Zerubbabel, saying Not by might, nor by power, but by my spirit, saith the Lord of hosts.*
>
> (*Zechariah 4:6*)

This verse lets us know we are engaged in a spiritual fight. The name Zerubbabel[9] means one who was born and descended from Babylon. Through Zerubbabel's name the LORD is saying, "those who were born in captivity will be restored and reborn by the spirit of the LORD."

This is a type between the children of Israel and the Body of Christ. It shows the characteristics that are shared between both groups of people. Each group is returning from captivity that has been caused by the growing desire for self-gratification and the lack of adherence to the Word of the LORD.

To leave Babylon we must change our way of thinking about the turbulent times that are being created. The errant behaviors and beliefs the world stresses are the catalyst that facilitates the people of the LORD to take their place in Him. Escaping from the confusion.

What is the destiny you are to fulfill? Find it by taking your place!

The book of Zechariah has a dual purpose as it walks us through Israel's process to restore worship and at the same time it has prophetic communications linked to the end time and our process of being redeemed by Christ fulfilling our destiny.

In verse three of chapter four it gives us a scene from the throne room of God. Where the two olive trees are clearly linked to the book of Revelation chapter 11 at the start of the tribulation.

> *And two olive trees by it, one upon the right side of the bowl, and the other upon the left side thereof.*
>
> *(Zechariah 4:3)*

> *These are the two olive trees, and the two candlesticks standing before the God of the earth.*
>
> *(Revelation 11:4)*

This displays the clear relationship between Zerubbabel's time and the time of the end linking it all to the throne room of the LORD. Revelation 11:1-2 mentions the measurement of the temple when it is restored in the tribulation period re-establishing the temple worship. Zerubbabel was in process of doing the same.

> *The hands of Zerubbabel have laid the foundation of this house; his hands shall also finish it; and thou shalt know that the LORD of hosts hath sent me unto you.*
>
> *For who hath despised the day of small things? For they shall rejoice, and shall see the plummet in the hands of Zerubbabel with those seven; they are the eyes of the LORD; which run to and fro through the whole earth.*
>
> *(Zechariah 4:9-10)*

Just as Zachariah was sent as a witness to Israel; the Lord Jesus Christ is in the throne room watching all that is happening in the earth.

> *And I beheld, and, lo, in the midst of the throne and*
> *of the four beasts, and in the midst of the elders,*
> *stood a Lamb as it had been slain, having seven*
> *horns and seven eyes, which are the seven Spirits*
> *of God sent forth into all the earth.*
>
> *(Revelation 5:6)*

We can see how prophetic statements in Zechariah line up with New Testament prophecy (Zechariah 9:9 and Matthew 21:5-9 Jesus riding an ass; Chapter six both in Zechariah and Revelation the horses ride).

When God speaks something at times it seems it may not happen due to obstacles and challenges. The temple had been waiting at the foundation stage (Zechariah 4:9). Ezra chapter four lets us know a 14-year delay occurred after the foundation was finished.

The Samaritans wanted to help with the building of the temple because they said we seek your God. This is in line with the woman at the well in John 4:7-9.

Zerubbabel refused their help because they were not Israeli. The Church is also being asked to allow righteousness to be mixed with unrighteous beliefs and behaviors.

The Samaritans sent letters to the king asking for a search to be made accusing Jerusalem of being a rebellious city and convincing him to stop the construction.

Does this sound familiar? Satan accuses the brethren of Jesus day and night before God bringing up our failures to cause a stoppage of our support from God (Revelation 12:10). He also plants thoughts in the mind of any person thinking of deciding to follow Christ. Doubt and fear of life changes erupts causing uncertainty.

Leave Babylon and walk through the challenges and distractions along the way, but don't be a person who complains about the journey. Challenges are your steppingstones to take your rightful position in Christ. The only thing that can stop you is yourself. Tell satan to get behind you (Matthew 4:1-11)!

He can't stop you from leaving Babylon and entering the fulness of Christ through the uncovering and unveiling of the testimony of Jesus Christ the redeemer of your life.

> *The Revelation of Jesus Christ, which God gave unto him, to shew unto his servants things which must shortly come to pass; and he sent and signified it by his angel unto his servant John;*
>
> *Who bare record of the word of God, and of the testimony of Jesus Christ, and of all things that he saw.*
>
> *Blessed is he that readeth, and they that hear the words of this prophecy, and keep those things which are written therein: for the time is at hand.*
>
> *(Revelation 1:1-3)*

We gain a full understanding of Christ through divine inspiration by the Spirit of God. It will guide us, showing all that is available through Christ.

The scriptures in chapters two and three of Revelation are for the purpose of warning what will come to pass in the church. This prophecy begins with the seven churches of that day. Like-wise the Body of Christ will be examined in the same manor before Jesus returns.

It's all about Jesus being revealed in our hearts, causing us to stand in confidence knowing our behavior is pleasing to God. Be not shaken by word or troubled in mind by what you see happening amongst Believers.

Here are some of the challenges for those churches:

- Ephesus – left first love
- Smyrna – will have tribulation, but be faithful unto death
- Pergamos – they dwell where satan's seat is entertaining people that hold the doctrine of Balaam (same doctrine when Israel went into captivity of Babylon) and the doctrine of the Nicolaitanes (linked to Balaam worship which is also linked to Nim'rod)
- Thyatira – suffered false teachers with teachings of committing fornication and serving idols
- Sardis – a name that they live but are dead
- Philadelphia – has little strength, but keeps the word of God and doesn't deny Christ's name; by keeping the word of His patience; they will be kept from the hour of temptation that comes to try them that dwell on the earth
- Laodiceans – neither cold nor hot; because lukewarm they will be spued out of the Lord's mouth; increased in goods but wretched, miserable, poor, blind and naked

The Babylonian culture was in the first century church. As the book of Ecclesiastes states, "there is no new thing under the sun. What is hath already been of old time, which was before."

> *For the time is come that judgment must begin at the house of God: and if it first begin at us, what shall the end be of them that obey not the gospel of God?*
>
> *(1 Peter 4:17)*

The same culture will be present in the churches at the end of time. We should keep the positive cultural reports from the seven churches and leave behind those behaviors and cultures that resemble a falling away from Christ.

Christ said to the church of Philadelphia, "keep the word of His patience and He would keep them from the hour of temptation." Patience[10] means to abide under. Temptation[11] means experience gained by divinely permitted trials with a purpose for a specific benefit.

Jesus is telling the Philadelphians because you abided under the Word of the LORD demonstrating endurance and did not denying Christ; therefore, you will be kept from the final trial to test the rest of the earth.

Doesn't this sound like the catching away of the Disciples of Jesus to meet Him in the air?

As time passes after we first believed in Christ, there is a tendency to become more and more desensitized of the events in our lives. The excellence and good within us begins to weaken. When this happens recognize it and act to correct it through repentance.

> *According as his divine power hath given unto us all things that pertain unto life and godliness, through the knowledge of him that hath called us to glory and virtue:*
>
> *Whereby are given unto us exceeding great and precious promises: that by these ye might be partakers of the divine nature, having escaped the corruption that is in the world through lust.*
>
> *(2 Peter 1:3-4)*

When you become desensitized your perspective of service to the LORD becomes less and less finite. Our perception begins to broaden as to what is acceptable and what is not.

> *Enter ye in at the strait gate: for wide is the gate,*
> *and broad is the way, that leadeth to destruction,*
> *and many there be which go in there at:*
>
> *(Matthew 7:13)*

The Word of the LORD warns all people to prevent them from being seduced into falsehood avoiding destruction. If we understand the testimony of Jesus and the spirit of prophecy it will keep us in a state of semi-revival being renewed each day. The question is does your current belief system fit or align with any of the churches mentioned in chapters two or three of Revelation?

Most Believers do not think of what they do as being linked to falsehood or unbelief; honest or dishonest. Are your thoughts aligned with the LORD? The Holy Spirit speaks to your subconscious evaluating the soul creating thoughts to reveal the legitimacy of our actions.

How is your thought life? Do any convictions from the Word enter your mind? I'm not talking about fear; I'm talking about thoughts that reveal where you are spiritually. This is a good place to start to gauge where you are.

Have you accepted Christ? Maybe you have never accepted Christ; maybe you accepted Christ and now are in a period where your beliefs are weakening.

Whatever state you are in call on Jesus and He will liberate you!

KEY THOUGHTS PAGE

Seek to Hear

Are you a babe in Christ? Some of us have a close relationship with Christ and there are people that have no experience with Christ. The goal for us all is the same. To possess the ability to hear what God is saying to us.

Understanding how to hear God is the starting and ending point. It is Christ speaking to us through the Spirit.

We can't change unless we are able to hear the Word of God with conviction.

> *And he spake many things unto them in parables, saying, Behold, a sower went forth to sow;*
>
> *And when he sowed, some seed fell by the way side, and the fowls came and devoured them up:*
>
> *Some fell upon stony places, where they had not much earth: and forthwith they sprung up, because they had no depth of earth:*

And when the sun was up, they were scorched; and because they had no root, they withered away.

And some fell among thorns; and the thorns sprung up, and choked them:

But other fell into good ground, and brought forth fruit, some an hundredfold, some sixtyfold, some thirtyfold.

Who hath ears to hear, let him hear.

(Matthew 13:3-9)

See Matthew 13:18-23 for explanation of this parable.

To hear[12] is to give audience (listen to), to report, and to understand. It is having the needed perception to discern the meaning of what is said. "Faith comes by hearing and hearing by the Word of God" (Romans 10:17).

After you understand the meaning of what's said, decide to accept it. Then your faith will be increased through the message the Word presents. The above parable gives us the image of what happens in the mind, soul, and spirit; the heart of a person when they hear the Word of God.

For the word of God is quick, and powerful, and sharper than any twoedged sword, piercing even to the dividing asunder of the soul and spirit, and of the joints and marrow, and is a discerner of the thoughts and intents of the heart.

(Hebrews 4:12)

The mind through our hearing capabilities receives the message but what's in our heart can impact how it is interpreted.

Here is a list of challenges for receiving the Word of God:

- Unable to understand the Word; therefore, it is easily dismissed
- Unbelief as the Word is spoken; it's just not feasible
- Offended when our beliefs are challenged
- Hidden things in our hearts that stops growth
  - holding on to things that bruised us causing the Word to have no effect
  - anger, prejudice, unforgiveness
- Concerns and other priorities become our focus and we don't seek the true bread of life, the true avenue for resources

All these challenges hinder the life of Christ to shine light into our hearts and allows darkness to remain.

In him was life; and the life was the light of men.

And the light shineth in darkness; and the darkness comprehended it not.

(John 1:4-5)

Darkness hinders the ability to perceive and understand. It stops us from seeing spiritually and at times makes it impossible to comprehend truth. "If the light in us is darkness how great is the darkness" (Matthew 6:23)?

The Spirit illuminates the heart to things pertaining to eternal life. The intent of our heart hinders the capability to possess, lay hold of, or own the benefits of eternal life. Causing an inability to hear and receive the Word. Is the Word of God growing and baring fruit in your life?

When you accept Jesus as savior. You are accepting the Word of God to be operative in your life.

> *And the Word was made flesh, and dwelt among us, (and we beheld his glory, the glory as of the only begotten of the Father,) full of grace and truth.*
>
> *(John 1:14)*

Let His Word fall on good ground. Mix it with faith as you open your heart. Are you seeking to learn what God is speaking to you? Make His Word and the promise of His life your priority.

The Disciples of Jesus will not develop the needed spiritual exchanges between them and God by simply understanding Biblical principles. The urgency of learning the spiritual reality of who we are in Christ makes the difference.

> *Blessed is the man that walketh not in the counsel of the ungodly, nor standeth in the way of sinners, nor sitteth in the seat of the scornfull.*
>
> *But his delight is in the law of the LORD; and in his law doth he meditate day and night.*
>
> *And he shall be like a tree planted by the rivers of water, that bringeth forth his fruit in his season; his leaf also shall not wither; and whatsoever he doeth shall prosper.*
>
> *(Psalms 1:1-3)*

Prepare for the battle that is ahead. Don't become bitter or angry at what you see around you, prosperity will come through meditating upon His Word. I'm speaking of spiritual prosperity resulting in your needs being met.

Are you able to hear the LORD's voice through meditation on the Word? Is He only seen as being your provider? The goal is for us to be in the place where He is revealing Himself as the eternal God?

"Birds neither work nor toil, yet God provides their needs" (Matthew 6:26). Your needs are a given if you are being a good steward of your resources. Desires can't be the focus of our relationship with Him.

The distinction between provider and eternal God of god's is important. The LORD transitioned from being El[13] (God) Shadday[14] (Almighty) the provider of grace, mercy, and riches (our provider) to revealing Himself as the God of gods, self-existent, and eternal God of all (Exodus 6:3).

When the word LORD is capitalized in most of the Old Testament it is referencing Jehovah[15] (Yahweh) the self-existent or eternal God. Because the Israeli people would not pronounce the word aloud, they used Adon[16] meaning master or Lord as well as Adonay[17] (Yahweh) the proper divine name used to signify God of gods and LORD over all.

This name transition was in a time of deliverance of the people of Israel from Egypt. Liberation is what was happening in Zechariah's time (from Babylon) and is happening now for us (from the world).

In times of transition the LORD shows the world He is the only supreme deity. We must be attentive to be able to see what He is doing in the spirit realm. "For we wrestle not against flesh and blood, but against principalities, against powers, against the rulers of the darkness of this world" (Ephesians 6:12).

I felt this was important because spiritual influences are increasing clearly showing that we are in a time of transition. Every person that says the word god may not be talking about the true God. An example is some people say, "the higher power." Are they talking about the LORD? This is all about recognition of who is speaking and under what authority. The LORD's sheep hear His voice.

The changing of Joshua's garments that occurred in Zechariah 3:3-4 as the preparation the LORD was making to transition him in the spirit realm for the role he would have. There are two acronyms I use related to hearing God to obtain a change of our garments during the transition. They are ASK and HELP.

How do you find something that you're not looking for; start the search "ASK (understanding of Christ) for HELP (through demonstration)"!

- A – Ask, and it shall be given you
- S – Seek, and ye shall find
- K – Knock and it shall be opened unto you

The acronym ASK is from Matthew 7:7. For us to learn to be led by the Spirit, we must walk in the light of God each day. Spend time practicing ASK.

> *Search the scriptures; for in them ye think ye have eternal life: and they are they which testify of me (Jesus).*
>
> *(John 5:39)*

We ASK by searching for understanding to walk in the newness of life through Christ Jesus.

- Ask – a person only asks for something they desire
  - seeking wisdom
  - to be born of the Spirit to overcome the world and keep His commandments
  - to walk with Him each day

- Seek – is an investigation to fill the craving to know the Lord Jesus
  - it is a search for the things above where Christ sits at the right hand of God (heavenly things)
  - coming to God believing He is and that He will reward those who diligently seek Him
- Knock – as you knock seeking entrance into His Kingdom
  - listen for His voice and open the door to you heart

For every one that asketh receiveth; and he that seeketh findeth; and to him that knocketh it shall be opened.

(Matthew 7:8)

How passionate are you about your relationship with Christ? Are you ASK'ing and listening to hear His response?

The goal of ASK is:

Not to be conformed to this world: but be ye transformed by the renewing of your mind, that ye may prove what is that good, and acceptable, and perfect, will of God.

(Romans 12:2)

The word mind[18] in this verse is our *consciousness* (heart and soul). How the intellect perceives and understands our thoughts, feelings, and will (the reasoning process). Renewing the mind requires self-reflection and meditation on the things of God to impact the heart as you listen for God's voice.

Let this mind be in you, which was also in Christ Jesus:

(Philippians 2:5)

The word mind[19] in this verse is the act of *exercising* the mind to think in a certain way. You must practice to a line your mind with the Word of God. If the word says you are a new creature in Christ, if it says you are the righteousness of God through Christ; then speak the Word to cause your thoughts to connect with the truth. There is a war between the mind and the soul (our heart).

> *For I delight in the law of God after the inward man:*
>
> *But I see another law in my members, warring against the law of my mind, and bringing me into captivity to the law of sin which is in my members.*
>
> *(Romans 7:22-23)*

The word mind in this verse is our consciousness (heart and soul). Our members[20] are the physical body that responds to the old stimulus. Wanting to fulfill sensual longings, causing the new person to be attacked through fulfilling the flesh.

Renewing of the mind is an internal change of our consciousness (heart) that influences our intellect in the way the subconscious makes judgements in the light of the will of God. This creates a change of thoughts and feelings triggering us to line up with Him. Jesus transforms you being your HELP through the Holy Spirit!

HELP is an acronym for hope, experience, love, and patience.

- H – "for we are saved by *hope*: but hope that is seen is not hope: for what a man seeth, why doth he yet hope for? But if we hope for that we see not, then do we with patience wait for it" (Romans 8:24-25)

Hope is anticipation with belief of a favorable outcome. It goes hand in hand with faith. Whatever you desire salvation, healing, deliverance, or an outcome in a life event; wait for it with hope. Knowing with confidence it will work out for your good.

> *Hope maketh not ashamed; because the love of God is shed abroad in our hearts by the Holy Ghost which is given unto us.*
>
> *(Romans 5:5)*

> *Now the God of hope fill you with all joy and peace in believing, that ye may abound in hope, through the power of the Holy Ghost.*
>
> *(Romans 15:13)*

- E – "patience, *experience*; and experience, hope:" (Romans 5:4)

Experience is the key to developing patience and hope. As we travel life's journey the test, trails, and victories we encounter allows us to build and to prove our trust in the Lord as our deliverer.

> *I will love thee, O Lord, my strength.*
>
> *The Lord is my rock, and my fortress, and my deliverer; my God, my strength, in whom I will trust; my buckler, and the horn of my salvation, and my high tower.*
>
> *(Psalms 18:1-2)*

Only through experience do we come to know and love God in this manner. Learn to recognize when God is using your life's events as tools for your development.

- L – "to know the *love* of Christ, which passeth knowledge, that ye might be filed with all the fulness of God" (Ephesians 3:19)

We must come to know God's affection, His love based on the essential nature He possess. A true sense of caring, benevolence, and compassion for people.

> *And the fulness have all we received, and grace for grace.*
>
> *(John 1:16)*

The fulness of God is the favor given us because of His graciousness. His influence toward us because His grace drives us to act and live in a way that His love is clearly seen in our actions. We become like Him able to understand the pain of others. Then we can truly be filed with His fulness.

- P – "to them who by *patient* continuance in well doing seek for glory and honour and immortality, eternal life:" (Romans 2:7).

Being patient[21] is endurance and consistency no matter what state you find yourself. It causes your actions to create glory and honor to God and demonstrates the existence of immortality and eternal life operating in you.

> *Not that I speak in respect of want: for I have learned, in whatsoever state I am, therewith to be content.*
>
> *(Philippians 4:11)*

Contentment is the true demonstration of patience.

HELP causes us to demonstrate the will of God through our actions. The world can see through our behavior and our confidence that *hope* in God seeks a favorable outcome because of the *experiences* we have had with Him being our strength and deliverer. God's *love* through caring and compassion for others is demonstrated as we show consistency no matter what is happening around us showing *patience* because our faith lies in the LORD of hosts through Jesus Christ.

ASK and HELP gives us the ability to act after we hear God.

> *Yea, a man may say, Thou hast faith, and I have*
> *works: shew me they faith without thy works, and*
> *I will shew thee my faith by my works.*
>
> *(James 2:18)*

God's capability to intercede in our lives as we do the work assigned to us is more operative than ever. You are the key to allowing Him to use your life.

As you progress through the stages of ASK and HELP you will discover that the Holy Spirit is not limited only to confirming our salvation. This is not the last destination for us.

> *That ye would walk worthy of God, who hath called*
> *you unto his kingdom and glory.*
>
> *(1 Thessalonians 2:12)*

Salvation is just the beginning. As we grow, we can demonstrate what Kingdom living is all about. "For the kingdom of God is not in word, but in power" (1 Corinthians 4:20).

Kingdom living is the demonstration of the power of God in our lives. The purpose of hearing God with clarity is to:

- Reveal "His will in earth as it is in heaven" (Matthew 6:10)
- Fulfill every promise, He has given from His throne in heaven
- Know all things are possible with God through our Lord Jesus Christ

And in that day ye shall ask me nothing. Verily, verily, I say unto you, Whatsoever ye shall ask the Father in my name, he will give it you.

Hiterto have ye asked nothing in my name: ask, and ye shall receive, that your joy may be full.

These things have I spoken unto you in proverbs: but the time cometh, when I shall no more speak unto you in proverbs, but I shall shew you plainly of the Father.

(John 16:23-25)

Jesus explained Kingdom living to the disciples. By communicating He would be leaving. Yet, they were assured at the time of His departure they had asked nothing of Him (in His name). After He leaves, they could have direct relationship with the Father and ask what they will of the Father in His name, and it would be given to them.

Recognize the power of the name of Jesus. Understand the Father (His attributes and personality) as you work your path forward. The Spirit of God will provide direct communication with a full awareness of the LORD through divine inspiration, through access to Him.

Jesus, when he had cried again with a loud voice, yielded up the ghost.

And, behold, the veil of the temple was rent in twain from the top to the bottom; and the earth did quake, and the rocks rent;

(Matthew 27:50-51)

Access to the Holy of Holies of God was provided at the death of Jesus the Christ, which rent the veil giving us admittance to God's throne. Step into the fullness of your testimony. Confirm who you are in Christ through actions.

For ye are the temple of the living God; as God hath said, I will dwell in them, and walk in them; and I will be their God, and they shall be my people.

(2 Corinthians 6:16)

Can you imagine what it really means to be the temple of God. All through history people only looked for God when life got challenging not realizing their position in Him. Sometimes struggles brings revival as a result. Many believe this is where we are right now; that revival is coming!

Remember revival can only come when the hearts of the people are soft and pliable able to hear the voice of the LORD.

Look at Jonah, when he went to Nineveh to minister the words of the LORD the heart of the people turned and repented (Jonah 3:10). Then the LORD withheld judgement.

Now let's look at Habakkuk. Habakkuk cried to the LORD to save the people from violence and iniquity (Habakkuk 1:2-3). But the LORD in verses five and six told Habakkuk He would do a work that Habakkuk would not believe.

Instead of saving the people the LORD would raise up Nebuchadnezzar (the Chaldean) for judgement. Why, because the hearts of the government (their kings) nor the hearts of the people would turn. The LORD even called Nebuchadnezzar His servant (Jeremiah 25:9) to be used for the purpose of judgement toward Israel.

Is revival coming? One thing I know, revival must first start in the hearts of the people that make up the Body of Christ. Then it will come to the world. As the Body senses the urgency of the times and take its rightful place through sharing the gospel.

Moses experienced this urgency when he asked Pharaoh to let the people go. He didn't ask to let them go indefinitely. He asked to go three days journey into the wilderness to do sacrifice to the LORD our God (Exodus 3:18). I like this phrase "the LORD our God." Moses was saying, "to do sacrifice to Jehovah (eternal – God of gods) which is our God. Clarifying and distinguishing God from all the other gods in Egypt.

We as the people of God are in the process of our three-day journey passing through the wilderness a dry and barren place to obtain the promise. Receiving atonement and the right to be with Him in eternity.

Psalm 90:4 state a thousand years in the LORD's sight is but as yesterday (a day). It has been almost to 2000 years since Christ's resurrection. So, we are about to enter the third day after His resurrection. We will worship God on this third day just as Moses requested of Pharaoh. Our journey will continue to show evidence of the fulfillment of Christ in a more powerful way.

The LORD brought Israel out of the bondage of Egypt with signs and wonders. Will the evidence of the fulfillment of Christ be shown through signs and wonders? Is this the proof of our crossing into the next level spiritually?

Signs and wonders do not increase faith. Christ did many signs and wonders, yet the Pharisees wanted Christ to prove Himself at their request (Matthew 12:39) by showing a sign. Even Herod had hoped to see Christ perform a miracle in his presence (Luke 23:8).

The miracle working power of Christ did not convince either of these groups (Pharisees or Herod) to accept Christ and be saved. No, He was crucified at their hands. Seek Jesus, not signs or wonders! Yet, signs and wonders do have a place in the hierarchy of God.

> *And these signs shall follow them that believe; In my name they cast out devils; they shall speak with new tongues;*
>
> *They shall take up serpents; and if they drink any deadly thing, it shall not hurt them; they shall lay hands on the sick, and they shall recover.*
>
> *(Mark 16:17-18)*

I believe as we enter the third day the "Body of Christ" will be very effective in deliverance ministry. Ephraim was born to Joseph and Asenath after Pharoah orchestrated their union. Joseph called the child Ephraim because God had been fruitful unto him in the land of affliction.

We will soon see the capabilities mentioned in Mark 16:17-18 being demonstrated more frequently through the Disciples of Christ; in this land of affliction.

As Paul said:

> *And my speech and my preaching was not with enticing words of man's wisdom, but in demonstration of the Spirit and of power:*
>
> *That your faith should not stand in the wisdom of men, but in the power of God.*
>
> *(1 Corinthians 2:4-5)*

Your journey is the path to an inspired life through the Spirit.

> *That Christ may dwell in your hearts by faith; that ye, being rooted and grounded in love;*
>
> *May be able to comprehend with all saints what is the breadth, and length, and depth, and height;*
>
> *And to know the love of Christ, which passeth knowledge, that ye might be filled with all the fulness of God.*
>
> *(Ephesians 3:17-19)*

Are you able to hear what is being said in these verses? The love of Christ can't be described. It goes beyond understanding in its effort to fill us with the fulness of God.

> *Him that overcometh will I make a pillar in the temple of my God, and he shall go no more out: and I will write upon him the name of my God, and the name of the city of my God, which is new Jerusalem, which cometh down out of the heaven from my God: and I will write upon him my new name.*
>
> *(Revelation 3:12)*

This was written to the church of Philadelphia. They abided under the Word of the LORD with patience. Demonstrating endurance not denying Christ (Message #2), through the ability to hear God and be led by His Spirit.

"Behold, I come quickly: hold that fast which thou hast, that no man takes thy crown" (Revelation 3:11).

KEY THOUGHTS PAGE

MESSAGE #4
(A New Family)

Children of God

Have you considered what it means to be a member of God's family? This realization requires a mental address change. To recognize that this world is not home. Jesus said, "they are not of this world" (John 17:16). When this thought becomes reality all apprehension of our new family and residence will be eliminated. Opening the door to a spiritual mindset.

If a person comes to know Jesus as savior above the age of 30, it is more difficult for them to possess the childlike faith needed to obtain a spiritual mindset. Many go through life with a carnal mindset. Saved, but working things out themselves. Unable to realize the full benefit of being a royal priest with the authority of God the Father.

I heard a preacher say, "God told him to do a certain task that required funding." When asked, how he would get the funding, he responded, "that's God's business, my part is to act on what he said, and the funding will come." This comment does not mean to sit down and expect it to happen; nor does it mean to press forward and spend money you don't have. It means he is not working from a carnal mindset depending on what he knows or can see.

We must learn to move forward based on the guidance of the Holy Spirit. Causing doors to open, showing the way to make it happen. Don't work things out on your own. Let God lead you and the rest will work out. It may not be easy, but it will come to pass.

> *Because the carnal mind is enmity against God: for it is not subject to the law of God, neither indeed can be.*
>
> *(Romans 8:7)*

When I was a babe Romans 8:7 appeared to say, "my mind is the enemy of God." Therefore, I must work on my mind to line up with the law of God; to overcome sin and live a holy life.

Years later I realized my mind is not God's enemy. If my mind was the enemy of God; how then can I be a child of God? My mind may be in opposition to His laws or His will, but it is not His enemy. What's in the heart is what influences our minds. By the Spirit He works to help our hearts to line up with His reality. Thereby, changing the mind!

His laws are not just about sin, they are principles to live by. The principles that Christ lived by.

> *A new commandment I give unto you, That ye love one another; as I have loved you, that ye also love one to another.*
>
> *By this shall all men know that ye are my disciples, if ye have love one to another.*
>
> *(John 13:34-35)*

This is the greatest law of all. It fulfills all commandments. Laws are in place for the unjust to identify sin. Are all laws for the unjust? Look at the following laws:

- Law of faith – Romans 3:27
- Law of liberty – James 1:25
- Law of Righteousness – Romans 9:31
- Law of the Spirit giving life – Romans 8:2; John 6:63

If the mind is not subject to the law of God it means the enmity of heart has influenced the opposition. Therefore, effecting every law that God has in place for benefit or for reproof. The heart can nullify even the laws that are benefits from the sacrifice of Christ.

> Woe unto you, lawyers! For ye have taken away the key of knowledge: ye entered not in yourselves, and them that were entering in ye hindered.
>
> (Luke 11:52)

Jesus made this comment to the lawyers as He interacted with the scribes and Pharisees. Basically, they hinder true knowledge of service to God. By focusing on sin (self-righteousness) closing the door to knowing what life in Christ is all about. A life of love, faith, liberty, righteousness, and a spirit filled life. All these are benefits of being a "Child of God."

Let the Holy Spirit revive your heart which will generate the thought pattern of being an heir of God. The temple was a physical representation of a place to meet God. His glory would visit the people providing atonement. For the Disciple of Christ our body is the temple of the Holy Spirit therefore atonement has been satisfied and the place of worship is within us (1 Corinthians 6:19).

And said unto me, What sees thou? And I said, I have looked, and behold a candlestick all of gold, with a bowl upon the top of it, and his seven lamps thereon, and seven pipes to the seven lamps, which are upon the top thereof:

(Zechariah 4:2)

The mystery of the seven stars which thou sawest in my right hand, and the seven golden candlesticks. The seven stars are the angels (leaders) of the seven churches: and the seven candlesticks which thou sawest are the seven churches.

(Revelation 1:20)

Are the seven candlesticks in the tabernacle symbolism for the church with Christ in heaven? Oil flowed through the pipes to the bowls enabling the candle stands to be lit. The Holy Spirit fell on the people in Acts chapter two appearing as cloven tongues like as of fire (Acts 2:3-4). The images here are very clear. By the Spirit of God, we are in Christ Jesus and Christ is in heaven. We have a direct line of communication by the Spirit to God through Christ.

Even when we were dead in sins, hath quickened us together with Christ, (by grace ye are saved;)

And hath raised us up together, and made us sit together in heavenly places in Christ Jesus:

That in the ages to come he might shew the exceeding riches of his grace in his kindness toward us through Christ Jesus.

(Ephesians 2:5-7)

Your address change is the fact that you sit in heavenly places.

> *That the God of our Lord Jesus Christ, the Father of glory, may give unto you the spirit of wisdom and revelation in the knowledge of him:*
>
> *The eyes of your understanding being enlightened; that ye may know what is the hope of his calling, and what the riches of the glory of his inheritance in the saints,*
>
> *And what is the exceeding greatness of his power to us-ward who believe, according to the working of his mighty power,*
>
> *Which he wrought in Christ, when he raised him from the dead, and set him at his own right hand in the heavenly places,*
>
> *(Ephesians 1:17-20)*

God wants us to realize we must tie into the revelation knowledge of Christ to understand our inheritance.

> *For as many as are led by the Spirit of God, they are the sons of God.*
>
> *For ye have not received the spirit of bondage again to fear; but ye have received the Spirit of adoption, where by we cry, Abba Father.*
>
> *The Spirit itself beareth witness with our spirit, that we are the children of God.*
>
> *(Romans 8:14-16)*

Being led by the Spirit validates God as our Father. Abba[22] is a phrase that has a personal intimate connotation that shows unreasoning trust and confidence (like the word PaPa). An example of this was when Jesus was in Gethsemane' He prayed saying, "Abba, Father, all things are possible unto thee, take away this cup from me: nevertheless, not what I will, but what thou wilt" (Mark 14:36).

Jesus showed His humanity while at the same time He showed His personal intimate connection and unreasoning trust in the Father. Due to the love of God (a selfless love) that was within Him. We must come to understand God's love in this way.

> For as the Father raiseth up the dead, and quickeneth them; even so the Son quickeneth whom he will.
>
> For the Father judgeth no man, but hath committed all judgment unto the Son:
>
> (John 5:21-22)

> Verily, verily, I say unto you, He that believeth on me (Jesus), the works that I do shall he do also; and greater works than these shall he do; because I go unto my Father.
>
> (John 14:12)

These scriptures are the transfer of authority and power from the Father to the Son, then to us as Christ gives us the power of a resurrected life in Him (John 5:21). As Paul said, "who shall lay anything to the charge of God's elect? It is God that justifies (Romans 8:33).

As you seek to draw nearer to God you will be transformed into the person that God sees, as a member of His family.

Even so we, when we were children, were in bondage under the elements of the world:

But when the fulness of the time was come, God sent forth his Son, made of a woman, made under the law,

To redeem them that were under the law, that we might receive the adoption of sons.

And because ye are sons, God hath sent forth the Spirit of his Son into your hearts, crying, Abba, Father.

Wherefore thou art no more a servant, but a son; and if a son, then an heir of God through Christ.

(Galatians 4:3-7)

The Spirit of God changes our hearts in a way that we cry out to Him as being our Father. The purpose of the family of God is to use the gifts He has given us (becoming what God sees in you) to help the body of Christ mature.

Is the adoption into the family of God a reality to you?

KEY THOUGHTS PAGE

People of Wonder

What is the evidence of a person of faith with belief in Jesus Christ? Life experiences points to the LORD's wonder working power. Has a child recovered from a sickness? Were you delivered from some type of accident that would have been life threatening? Somehow when your finances were short the money seemed to stretch or the impossible happened on your job when there seemed to be no way for success. All these things are possible wonders performed at the hand of God. Everything does not occur by chance.

> *Hear now, O Joshua the high priest, thou, and thy fellows that sit before thee: for they are men wondered at: for, behold, I will bring forth my servant the BRANCH.*
>
> *(Zechariah 3:8)*

Can you see how the pattern in Zechariah 3:8 is for today? It is made clear in the last statement of the verse, *"I will bring forth my servant the BRANCH."* This is Jesus Christ; this prophecy is not only for Joshua to become priest during the rebuilding of the temple. It is a pattern (mirror image) of today for the people of God to rebuild our place of worship being in the presence of the LORD.

The word fellows[23] represents a close friend. A relationship best expressed as a relative or a very close companion. The word wondered[24] is the Hebrew word mowpheth (mo-faith) meaning to stand out, a sign, a miracle, by divine act or a special display of divine power. The pronunciation of the Hebrew word for wondered (mo-faith) is interesting. Yes, it will take faith and dependance on Christ for us to do what is required in this hour.

Here is a second witness from the book of Isaiah stating the people with him are for signs and wonders unto the people.

> *Behold, I and the children whom the LORD hath given me are for signs and for wonders in Israel from the LORD of hosts, which dwelleth in mount Zion.*
>
> *(Isaiah 8:18)*

Signs and wonders are special displays of divine acts from God. The invisibility of the power of God working through His people. To be a witness to the world that the LORD of hosts is God all alone.

Our witness is:

- the sacrifices of thanks and praise that allow us to share the gospel, untying the bands of wickedness
- healing the broken hearted, undoing heavy burdens
- proclaiming deliverance to captives, letting the oppressed go free
- recovery of site to the blind
- liberty to the bruised and bound, that breaks every yoke

This is our destiny! To display faith with confidence in God to deliver causing the world to wonder.

To be a person of wonder its more than the display of signs and wonders. It is important that a personality of consistency (no big highs and no big lows) is presented. Displaying peace in the mist of sorrow and distress. A person that inspires those around them to move forward in the mist of barriers. These attributes are of great value to the world as the Spirit of God works through us.

> *And when they shall say unto you, Seek unto them that have familiar spirits, and unto wizards that peep, and that mutter: should not a people seek unto their God? For the living to the dead?*
>
> *To the law and to the testimony: if they speak not according to this word, it is because there is not light in them.*
>
> *(Isaiah 8:19-20)*

God's people should not join with those who join themselves with such people. Just as Simon saw the gift of the Holy Ghost was given by the laying on of hands. He offered to give Peter money to receive the power to do the same (Acts 8:18-23). We must have a discerning eye and ear to understand what spirit is influencing what is said and what we see happening.

> *And no marvel; for satan himself is transformed into an angel of light.*
>
> *Therefore it is no great thing if his ministers also be transformed as the ministers of righteousness; whose end shall be according to their works.*
>
> *(2 Corinthians 11:14-15)*

There is always a counterfeit from satan. As the works of God are performed, there will also be people amazed by the supernatural practices of deception and wickedness. Getting advice from those who practice witchcraft and sorcery. Palm readers, people who chant calling the names of the dead to receive influence, and people who manipulates situations through deceit all fall into this category. Moses and Aaron experienced this in Exodus 7:10-12 (the casting down of the rods).

> For we wrestle not against flesh and blood, but against principalities, against powers, against the rulers of the darkness of this world, against spiritual wickedness in high places.
>
> *(Ephesians 6:12)*

Spiritual deception is going to be so great in the coming years it will become difficult to tell who are true and who are of the father of lies? Put on the armor of God to be able to stand against the wiles of satan. He will not always be in open challenge to God. There will be deception making things seem acceptable that are against the Word of God.

- Walk - bind the gospel to your feet (the truth of Jesus) that you will have a firm footing as you walk not being deceived
- Faith - the shield that stops all the plans of the wicked that are fired at you (naturally and spiritually)
- Helmet - knowledge of salvation that keeps you from a doubting mind about your redemption (no matter what's happening in the world)
- Sword - the Word of God as your weapon; speak it in every situation

- Prayer - watch while you pray (do not let your prayers be misguided); make your request to God

Prayers sometimes can be misguided when they only focus on what's wanted or the perception of what's best. There are times when what we want is not the best thing and necessarily not God's will.

Most of us all hope for a higher quality of life. We pray for our government to improve and have a morally correct direction as they govern. A prayer like this may have some impact for some issues, but is it God's will to fix all the elements of this world government?

The future for God is to have a new heaven and a new earth (Revelation 21:1). Remember this is not your home. We should pray for those who govern, but how should we pray?

In this hour prayers should be focused on the will of God. His will is that none should parish and those whose heart is changed would walk in newness of life making different decisions. This goes for those in government also; LORD change the hearts of leaders. Pray about polices that are in direct conflict with the Word or will make it easier for deception to be accepted. Trust has been in the government; it should have been in God. After all Jesus is coming back to judge the world governments whose mentor is lawlessness.

There is a scene at the start of chapter three of Zechariah that illustrates where the Body of Christ is today. It is of Joshua being with and angel while satan resists him. The LORD rebukes satan and Joshua's filthy garments are taken away and new garments are provided.

This is a picture of satan challenging the right of us becoming righteous before God. Just as he was rebuked in Zechariah chapter three by the LORD. We can bind satan as we practice the principles in Ephesians 6:11-18 (the armor of God). This is an hour to deal with strongholds. Some strongholds may remain as we enter the time of sorrows leading to the catching away of the Body of Christ. Trust in the LORD and in the power of His might.

The battle of accusation and deceit happened in the garden, it happened to Job, and it will continue to happen until the end of time. Joshua[25] is the word Yhowshua (Yeshua) meaning Jehovah saves. Jesus[26] in Greek is the name for the Hebrew name Joshua. Jesus is the savior rebuffing the challenges of satan.

> *Greater love hath no man than this, that a man lay down his life for his friends.*
>
> *Ye are my friends, if ye do whatsoever I command you.*
>
> *Henceforth I call you not, servants; for the servant knoweth not what his lord doeth; but I have called you friends; for all things that I have heard of my Father I have made known unto you.*
>
> *(John 15:13-15)*

There are many questions relating to our interaction with God. Have the capabilities of God to intervene in our lives become inoperative? Is the job of the Holy Ghost now limited to conviction of salvation? Is salvation the last destination for us? Are signs and wonders necessary; are they even a possibility?

> *Verily, verily, I say unto you, He that believeth on me, the works that I do shall he do also; and greater works than these shall he do; because I go unto my Father.*
>
> *And whatsoever ye shall ask in my name, that will I do, that the Father may be glorified in the Son.*

If ye shall ask any thing in my name, I will do it.

If ye love me, keep my commandments.

And I will pray the Father, and he shall give you another Comforter, that he may abide with you for ever;

Even the Spirit of truth; whom the world cannot receive, because it seeth him not, neither knoweth him: but ye know him; for he dwelleth with you, and shall be in you.

I will not leave you comfortless: I will come to you.

(John 14:12-18)

Signs and wonders are still possible because Jesus said, "the works He did should also be done by those that believe on Him." God still intervenes for us because Jesus has prayed for us giving the gift of the Comforter (Holy Spirit) as a lead and guide. The Holy Spirit does more than confirm salvation it leads to all truth and bestows gifts unto us to help minister to the Body of Christ.

The issue with today's society is that the Holy Spirit is not abiding in most of the people. Many cannot see Him, and they don't want to know Him preventing understanding of the truth. An interesting thing is when a truth is refused, blame if flipped through constant repetition of stating the views contrary to the truth. Causing any who oppose to become the parties who are in error based on today's social norms.

Will new norms hinder the prophecy and the testimony of Jesus Christ? I believe the events of today are a catalyst to a change in mindset about the true reality of God and His purpose to be fulfilled through each of us.

Continuance of your journey will help discover some answers to becoming a people of wonder. The full power of God operating through the Holy Spirit as comforter, teacher, and guide; with signs and wonders becoming a part of your life as God wills.

Some of us have not thought much about the spiritual structure put in place by the LORD. Angels had interaction with the people in the Bible. There is an entire structure in the heavenlies at work every day as a benefit for the Disciples of Christ.

Tsaba[27] is the word for hosts meaning a host for the purpose of military service (an army) for the purpose of an organized campaign or war. These are the angels of the LORD.

> And when the servant of the man of God was risen early, and gone forth, behold, an host compassed the city both with horses and chariots. And his servant said unto him, Alas, my master! How shall we do?
>
> And he answered, Fear not: for they that be with us are more than they that be with them.
>
> And Elisha prayed, and said, LORD, I pray thee, open his eyes, that he may see. And the LORD opened the eyes of the young man; and he saw; and, behold the mountains was full of horses and chariots of fire round about Elisha.
>
> (2 Kings 6:15-17)

The above verses are a result of the king of Syria sending solders to take Elisha prisoner. This is an example of the reality of the following scriptures.

For he will give his angels charge over thee, to keep thee in all thy ways.

(Psalms 91:11)

And of the angels he saith, Who maketh his angels spirits, and his ministers a flame of fire.

(Hebrews 1:7)

Are they not all ministering spirits, sent forth to minister for them who shall be heirs of salvation?

(Hebrews 1:14)

Ministers[28] in Hebrews 1:7 denotes angels being sent forth to support and serve the Disciples of Christ. Fire[29] signifying the holiness of God and angels as ministers sent to help fulfill His will.

Take your place. Make the next year a year of difference for good through divine inspiration and power.

KEY THOUGHTS PAGE

Mountain Movers

*Yea doubtless, and I count all things but loss for
the excellency of the knowledge of Christ Jesus my
Lord:*

(*Philippians 3:8*)

Believers should progress in understanding to gain the full
knowledge of Christ. Demonstration comes *through observation
and experience* as we seek to know the savior in all areas of our life.

*According as his divine power hath given unto
us all things that pertain unto life and godliness,
through the knowledge of him that hath called us
to glory and virtue:*

*Whereby are given unto us exceeding great and
precious promises: that by these ye might be
partakers of the divine nature, having escaped the
corruption that is in the world through lust.*

(*2 Peter 1:3-4*)

For so an entrance shall be ministered unto you abundantly into the everlasting kingdom of our Lord and Saviour Jesus Christ.

(2 Petter 1:11)

God's divine power has given the knowledge that allows glory and virtue to manifest the nature of God making our calling and election sure. The word Kingdom[30] is the realm of sovereignty, of royal power, and dominion of God. This starts here on earth as we procure the needed valor to usher us to new levels of Kingdom living through our Lord and Savior Jesus Christ.

Are you entering new levels of Kingdom living? A place where the power within overcomes mountains (obstacles) occurring to hinder you? A mountain is anything that is in the way of accomplishing God's will naturally or spiritually.

Who art thou, O great mountain? Before Zerubbabel thou shalt become a plain: and he shall bring forth the headstone thereof with shoutings, crying, Grace, grace unto it.

(Zechariah 4:7)

For verily I say unto you, That whosoever shall say unto this mountain, Be thou removed, and be thou cast into the sea, and shall not doubt in his heart, but shall believe that those things which he saith shall come to pass; he shall have whatsoever he saith.

Therefore I say unto you, What things soever ye desire, when ye pray, believe that ye receive them, and ye shall have them.

(Mark 11:23-24)

These two examples of dealing with mountains shows we must understand the power we have. Both occurrences are rooted in the natural and the spiritual.

Zerubbabel is facing opposition to completing the temple. There are natural challenges associated with any building project and there are spiritual challenges from the Samaritans being used by satan to hinder the construction. Sometimes we don't realize opposition from people are instruments of satan.

Mark 11:23-24 are linked to Jesus walking up to the fig tree to obtain some fruit, but there was none. If a fig tree had leaves fruit should have been present. Jesus then cursed the tree because it was out of line with God's natural order. Naturally the tree had no fruit, but spiritually it looked the part by having leaves. If we look the part, we should bare the fruit also.

> *I am the vine, ye are the branches: He that abideth in me, and I in him, the same bringeth forth much fruit: for without me ye can do nothing.*
>
> *If a man abide not in me, he is cast fourth as a branch, and is withered; and men gather them, and cast them into the fire, and they are burned.*
>
> *(John 15:5-6)*

Just as the fig tree withered (Mark 11:21) we will also, if we don't produce fruit by abiding in Christ. Non-activity causes us to be complacent. Many times, we give the natural things (see, touch, taste) more weight than the might of the invisible things of the Spirit.

The key to moving mountains as you pray; is to speak what God says about them from His Word.

When speaking to concur mountains, is belief the same as faith? The Greek word pistis is the same word for belief in 2 Thessalonians 2:13 and faith in Hebrews 11:1.

> *Now faith is the substance of things hoped for, the evidence of things not seen.*
>
> *For by it the elders obtained a good report.*
>
> *Through faith we understand that the worlds were framed by the word of God, so that things which are seen were not made of things which do appear.*
>
> *(Hebrews 11:1-3)*

The word faith[31] (pistis) is having a conviction (being firmly convinced) and persuaded about something. Your ability to believe creates the substance that causes the thing to take form becoming a reality. In the natural some would say, "it seems to have worked out."

In Mark 11:23 Jesus said, "if you don't doubt in your heart and believe what you say it will come to pass." The Greek word here for believe is pisteuo to accept as true even if you don't see it. The words convinced (pistis) and accept (pisteuo) convey two different things.

I accept (pisteuo) that a one-ton truck can hold a lawn mower, but I display pistis when I am firmly convinced in my heart when I believe something is reality that I can't see or haven't seen before.

After you have the conviction being firmly convinced in your heart (pistis) accept that your request is reality (pisteuo). The substance of your request appears when God works supernaturally or through the natural to bring it to reality.

> *Jesus said unto him, If thou canst believe, all things are possible to him the believeth.*

> *And straightway the father of the child cried out,*
> *and said with tears, Lord, I believe, help thou mine*
> *unbelief.*
>
> (Mark 9:23-24)

The father of the child with the dumb and deaf spirit believed (pisteuo). Accepted that Jesus could heal from prior demonstrations of His power. But, asked for help with his unbelief because of an element of faithlessness not knowing He would. Basically, his unbelief is similar to knowing something can happen, but you are not sure it will.

I heard Billy Graham say in a message, "many of us believe Jesus is real with our minds, but the question is do you believe on Jesus in a way that you make Him Lord?" Is Jesus the reality of your faith, thereby giving Him Lordship?

Faith comes by hearing, and hearing by the Word of God! Belief crosses over into faith when our mental confidence moves into a reality of the heart as we place it with unwavering assurance at the feet of Jesus.

> *Ye also, as lively stones, are built up a spiritual*
> *house, an holy priesthood, to offer up spiritual*
> *sacrifices, acceptable to God by Jesus Christ.*
>
> (1 Peter 2:5)

Offering scarifies of praise, giving of thanks, and prayers of deliverance to God creates the reality that regenerates us through His presence enabling us to move forward to resolve every issue.

Christ sits at the right hand of God making intercession for us (Romans 8:26-27; 34) joining in with every request. Making petition to God on our behalf allowing prayers and offerings to be presented as we give thanks in the name of Jesus.

(As it is written, I have made thee a father of many nations,) before him whom he believed, even God, who quickeneth the dead, and calleth those things which be not as though they were.

(Romans 4:17)

Our view of the world challenges should be handled through our supplications endowed by the power of the LORD God through Christ. Allowing things that are not, to be spoken as if they were. Causing them to become reality.

And I sought for a man among them, that should make up the hedge, and stand in the gap before me for the land, that I should not destroy it; but I found none.

(Ezekiel 22:30)

The Lord is seeking for someone to stand in the gap for an unrighteous generation. Willing to speak to the issues of the day. Are you that person?

I WILL stand upon my watch, and set me upon the tower, and will watch to see what he will say unto me, and what I shall answer when I am reproved.

And the LORD answered me, and said, Write the vision, and make it plain upon tables, that he may run that readeth it.

For the vision is yet for an appointed time, but at the end it shall speak, and not lie: though it tarry, wait for it; because it will surely come, it will not tarry.

Behold, his soul which is lifted up is not upright in him: but the just shall live by his faith.

(Habakkuk 2:1-4)

After verse four Habakkuk begins to proclaim several woes because of behaviors and cultures that were present in the nation. Many of the same challenges are present today.

The appointed time is closer than ever. A time at the end when the people of the world (symbolically Babylon) press forward as one humanity causing the necessity of the just to live by faith. I am watching for God's appointed time in these last day's just as Habakkuk did when woes (sorrows) come upon this earth.

Accept your appointment. The Disciples in Act 4:29-31 in the mist of being threatened seek boldness to speak God's Word. Then the Holy Ghost came filling them for that appointed time. Just as Peter saw the lame man at the gate called "Beautiful" (Acts 3:2-7). The word beautiful[32] in verse two means seasonally produced at the right time and the right hour.

> *I pray not that thou shouldest take them out of the world, but that thou shouldest keep them from the evil.*
>
> *They are not of the world, even as I am not of the world.*
>
> *Sanctify them through thy truth: thy word is truth.*
>
> *As thou hast sent me into the world, even so have I also sent them into the world.*
>
> *And for their sakes I sanctify myself, that they also might be sanctified through the truth.*

> *Neither pray I for these alone, but for them also*
> *which shall believe on me through their word (this*
> *is us);*
>
> *(John 17:15-20)*

Jesus gave us the words of God allowing us to be sanctified in truth. Revealing the glory of God wherever we go at just the right moment.

The Bible tells us we overcome satan by the blood of the lamb (Jesus) and the word of our testimony (Revelation 12:11). So, I will share a couple of testimonies (witnesses of evidence).

I had a hernia, couldn't hardly move without pain. My grass was getting tall and I heard within me, "go cut the grass." I thought, "what, I can hardly move."

I tried and after a few steps went back in the house. A day or so later I heard within me again, "go cut the grass", then I knew it was the Spirit of God speaking to me and was firmly convinced in my heart allowing me to accept that my healing was happening.

We must try the spirit and know who is doing the talking. Every thought does not come from God, if it is not from Him, we shouldn't do it.

With confidence God was speaking to me I tried again and after making one path the pain worsened. I waited another day and tried again. This time while I was cutting the grass I looked and realized I had made two or three rounds and did not feel any pain (healed as I went). I began to praise God, "I am healed". I went to the doctor he didn't understand how it happened (most doctors won't).

I had another experience and needed a surgery, but had to wait six weeks. I prayed and seemed to get better then things got worse. After having the surgery there was complications appearing that there may have been a laceration of another organ causing the symptoms I was having.

One day as I got out of my recliner my wife said, "you said you believed God would heal you of this problem did He, or didn't He?" I know now my problem was the phrase, "He would heal me".

I sat back in the recliner and said, "Father I believe (pistis) your Word and I am healed of this problem in the name of Jesus." As I sat there the Holy Ghost moved on me and I replied, "thank you LORD for my healing." From that point on I got better and better until the doctor told me what they were seeing on the scans was gone.

Why didn't I receive the healing before the surgery? Was it because I was in process of making a wrong move in my career, so God allowed it because the surgery prevented the move; was it because of something within me before the surgery where my words were not mixed with faith, was I going through the motions? The answer is I don't know. I think it was a mix of things. Either way it was not because God couldn't do it.

My comment to you is speak what God say's about your situation and when the dust settles, know He is God no matter what the outcome.

All healings are not immediate (Mark 8:24-25). Jesus spit on the blind man's eyes and laid hands on him then asked him what he saw. After laying hands on him a second time and telling him to look up the man saw clearly.

The point is each healing may not be immediate and there is no set prescription for how it happens. It all depends on the variables relating to each situation.

We must act on what God tells us. But sometimes we pray and it seems nothing happened. There are times we look at our request as being in the future. Does this meet the criteria of faith?

Speak to the mountain! Have faith in God through Christ that His eternal purpose be revealed.

KEY THOUGHTS PAGE

MESSAGE #7

(LAST DAYS VISITATION)

End Times

The prior five messages were intended for you to consider your development in the Lord Jesus as the time of the end approaches.

We must leave Babylon, hear God, be heirs of God; possess divine inspiration and power; demonstrate God's will now and at the time of the end.

During these stressful times those who have some knowledge of God are wondering if the events of today are leading to Christ's return. This message is about the end time prophecy of Jesus in Matthew chapter 24. It will clarify events leading to Christ's return.

What does the return of Christ mean? The timing of His return is illustrated differently for each group depending on their belief system and the condition of their heart. There are illustrations in God's Word of the timing of Christ's return for His Disciples, the Israeli people, and those who are of the world.

My thoughts are the events in Matthew chapter 24 and the book of Revelation are in chronological order. This premise is what the rest of this chapter is based on.

As I move forward, please know there are scriptures relating to the Body of Christ and scriptures relating to Israel that seem similar when considering the end time prophecies; we must distinguish the difference between them to recognize for whom they are meant.

First, I'll discuss the Body of Christ:

> *For the Lord himself shall descend from heaven with a shout, with the voice of the archangel, and the trump of God: and the dead in Christ shall rise first:*
>
> *Then we which are alive and remain shall be caught up together with them in the clouds, to meet the Lord in the air: and so shall we ever be with the Lord.*
>
> (1 Thessalonians 4:16-17)

1 Thessalonians 4:16-17 is related to the Body of Christ. I know this because in verse 16 Paul mentions the dead in Christ and verse 17 he says, "we who are alive and remain shall be caught up." It is implied that those caught up are Disciples of Christ based on it being mentioned right after the dead in Christ being raised.

The people of Israel when this was written didn't believe in Jesus as Messiah. So, these scriptures can't be related to Israel, and it is not related to anyone who has rejected Christ.

Let's look at 2 Thessalonians 2:1-8:

> *Now we beseech you, brethren, by the coming of our Lord Jesus Christ, and by our gathering together unto him,*

That ye be not soon shaken in mind, or be troubled, neither by spirit, nor by word, nor by letter as from us, as that the day of Christ is at hand.

Let no man deceive you by any means: for that day shall not come, except there come a falling away first, and that the man of sin be revealed, the son of perdition;

Who opposeth and exalteth himself above all that is called God, or that is worshipped; so that he as God sitteth in the temple of God, shewing himself that he is God.

Remember ye not, that, when I was yet with you, I told you these things?

And now ye know what withholdeth that he might be revealed in his time.

For the mystery of iniquity doth already work: only he who now letteth will let, until he be taken out of the way.

And then shall that Wicked be revealed, whom the Lord shall consume with the spirit of his mouth, and shall destroy with the brightness of his coming:

(2 Thessalonians 2:1-8)

This is the second time Paul has written to the Thessalonians about the coming of Christ. There must have been debate still occurring about the return (verse two).

Verse one is a key verse; he said, "our gathering together unto him." The gathering to Christ must be Disciples. He is talking to Believers in this verse. Then in verse three he mentions a falling away. This must be a falling away of Believers because the Israeli nation can't fall away because they never believed in Christ as a whole.

Most Church members believe in pre-tribulation departure of Believers. The Body of Christ will be caught up prior to the tribulation period. But according to the end of verse three the man of sin must be revealed. Does this mean the Body of Christ is going through the tribulation? No, I define the tribulation period for the world as the events happening in the book of Revelation when the seven trumpets begin to sound in Revelation 8:6.

The trumpets preparing to sound in Revelations 8:6 is the signal for the Israeli people and the people who rejected Jesus to have the chance for repentance as they go through the tribulation period.

But it does mean the man that will become anti-christ will be in the earth prior to the Disciples of Christ being caught up. We will get an indication of who he is from events that occur at his hands (Revelation 6:2) as he presses for dominance and control.

Prior to Revelation chapter 11 the man that is to become the man of sin is a man simply seeking power and control even supporting Israel to re-establish the temple.

2 Thessalonians 2:6-7 give details relating to satan being cast down, the falling way, and the timing of the man of sin being revealed. The key is at the end of verse six; the phrase "what withholdeth[33] that he might be revealed in his time".

The word withholdeth means to hold fast and to hinder the progress. This makes me think God will hinder the progress of the man who seduces the world. So, what does the end of verse seven mean; "he who now letteth will let, until he be taken[34] out of the way." The difference is verse six speaks about the man pushing for control; verse seven is talking about satan.

Taken means to cause to be or become, to come into being, to be made. God will let things progress until the seductive man is replaced with satan causing him to become anti-christ (*he who opposes Christ)*. Hence satan is taken out of the way in the spiritual realm when Michael the archangel casts him to the earth (Revelation 12:7-9). Then anti-christ is revealed.

Some say these verses are related to the Holy Spirit; when the Spirit is gone then anti-christ is revealed; some say this is the Church being caught up because when the Church is gone the Holy Spirit is gone also.

This is where a phrase I have always said comes into play; "Our prior learning is what hinders us when it comes to our understanding of scripture."

The things we thought we understood puts up barriers to new revelations from the LORD. You can decide what the verses mean based on what I have shared or the knowledge you already have! Ask the Holy Spirit to guide you.

The falling away isn't something that happens overnight. It is already in progress. Verse three is what hinders the progress of the catching away and revealing of anti-christ. The Bride of Christ can't be caught up until the falling way happens.

If we make verse four a part of the description of the son of perdition, then the verses would read this way:

> *Let no man deceive you by any means; for that day shall not come, except there come a falling away first, and the man of sin be revealed, the son of perdition; opposing and exalteth himself above all that is called God; shewing himself that he is God.*
>
> *Remember ye not, that, when I was with you, I told you these things?*
>
> *And now ye know what withholdeth that he might be revealed in his time.*
>
> *(2 Thessalonians 3 (modified) -6)*

Reading it this way what withholdeth is linked to the falling away. The falling away is what hinders the son of perdition from being revealed in his time.

When Jesus comes unbelief and turmoil is occurring among His people. Causing confidence in God to be shaken because of what is being witnessed on earth. We must endure until the end (Matthew 24:13).

The falling away seems to be an avenue to divide the sheep from the goats and the tares from the wheat finalizing the selection of those to be caught up. Or, did the mystery of iniquity that was at work in verse seven cause it?

A mystery[35] is something outside the range of natural apprehension. It takes divine revelation for it to be known at the appointed time.

> *Every tree that bringeth not forth good fruit is hewn down, and cast into the fire.*
>
> *Wherefore by their fruits ye shall know them.*
>
> *Not every one that saith unto me, Lord, Lord, shall enter into the Kingdom of heaven; but he that doeth the will of my Father which is in heaven.*
>
> *Many will say to me in that day, Lord, Lord, have we not prophesied in thy name? and in thy name have cast out devils? And in thy name done many wonderful works?*
>
> *And then will I profess unto them, I never knew you: depart from me, ye that work iniquity.*
>
> (Matthew 7:19-23)

Iniquity as used in Matthew 7:23 is the violation of the known laws of God. This means it can only be performed by people who are aware that what they do is a violation. Yet they are deceived into thinking it is not critical to God if they do it.

The people who believed they were of Christ spoken of in these verses must have fallen to iniquity! This would seem to be outside of natural apprehension. How could this happen?

Iniquity are wicked influences for the purpose of deceiving God's people and all of mankind. Didn't Paul say in 2 Corinthians 11:14-15, "not to marvel that satan is transformed into an angel of light. That it's not a great thing his ministers would also be transformed as the ministers of righteousness." This is why Jesus said, "you would know them by their fruit." Do they display fruit of righteousness?

Iniquity has always been in the earth look at its influence on Adam and Eve. God told them they would die if they ate the fruit. But they were influenced to do it anyway (Genesis 3:2-5) by the serpent that was used of satan.

What was the iniquity[36] that influenced these Believers?

Obviously, the people Jesus spoke to in Matthew 7:23 had a form of disobedience; they must have been acting contrary to the laws of God even though they believed in the reality of Christ (this is the essence of iniquity).

They understood the power of the name of Jesus and at some point, believed they were converted. Why else would Jesus say, "not everyone that says Lord, Lord will enter heaven; only those who do the will of His Father will enter" (Matthew 7:21).

Maybe that's why it's a mystery. Only the Spirit knows the heart of each person on the earth; their intent and motivation behind what they do.

> *Having a form of godliness, but denying the power thereof: from such turn away.*
>
> *(2 Timothy 3:5)*

The verses prior and after 2 Timothy 3:5 lists behaviors that even the lay Christian would feel inappropriate. These persons had an outward appearance of godliness[37] of having a godward attitude well pleasing to God. The behaviors of their lives contradicted the ability of God to change their heart.

Our own individual desires are what creates iniquity. Don't let experiences or perceptions harbor within; over ruling what is learned from the LORD. Doing this allows acceptance of falsehoods that line up with the errant beliefs. Thereby, justifying yourself for accepting them.

Believing about Christ does not mean you are a child of God!

> *Thou believest that there is one God; thou doest well: the devils also believe, and tremble.*
>
> *But wilt thou know, O vain man, that faith without works is dead?*
>
> *(James 2:19-20)*

All gifts and callings of God are without repentance (Romans 11:29). God called Israel to be His people and they turned their backs on Him. That doesn't change the fact that He called them as His people. You have a choice!

> *For the time is come that judgment must begin at the house of God: and if it first begin at us, what shall the end be of them that obey not the gospel of God?*
>
> *And if the righteous scarcely be saved, where shall the ungodly and the sinner appear?*

> *Wherefore let them that suffer according to the will*
> *of God commit the keeping of their souls to him in*
> *well doing as unto a faithful Creator.*
>
> (1 Peter 4:17-19)

These verses in Luke marry nicely with the last verse above.

> *And ye shall be hated of all men for my name's sake.*
>
> *But there shall not an hair of your head perish.*
>
> *In your patience possess ye your souls.*
>
> (Luke 21:17-19)

The last verse in 1 Peter and the last verse in Luke above are encouraging us to be patient in the coming days to display endurance and consistency as we abide in Christ. By doing so we can possess[38] procure the mastery of our souls[39]; this is a must for survival to endure the last days. Doing all we can to keep the Spirit of God working in us guarding our souls against iniquity.

2 Thessalonians 2:4, 8 are related to Israel and the anti-christ. These verses are related to Israel because they point to the abomination of desolation which occurs in the second half of the tribulation. The Body of Christ is caught up before this happens.

Tribulations first three and a half years starts in Revelation 11:1-2 when Israel has a treaty with anti-christ and the temple worship is started causing the need for the two witnesses to give testimony of the true plan of God to the world.

Revelation 12:6 starts the second three and a half years during the seven-year tribulation. This is when the desolation of the temple happens that was mentioned in Matthew 24:15 and 2

Thessalonians 2:4 occurring in Revelation 13:6-7. Christ second coming is after the working of satan with signs and lying wonders (Revelations 13:13-14) for the Israeli people.

There are two comings of Jesus the Christ for His people; the first coming occurs in Revelation chapter seven after the 144,000 of the tribes of Israel were sealed then the Body of Christ is caught up as the great multitude that came out of tribulation (sorrows) (Revelation 7:9-14).

The second coming is in Revelation chapter 14 when the 144,000 of the tribes of Israel that were sealed in chapter seven return with Christ for those Israeli's who now realize Jesus is their Messiah and any others in the world who have repented (Revelation 14:1-16).

Below I submit to you a table linking Matthew chapter 24 to other scriptures that relates to the "end times". The table is much simpler for you to review.

The evidence of Jesus being Lord of all comes through the Spirit foretelling and predicting to the world the events of the end time. For the testimony of Jesus is the spirit of prophecy (Revelation 19:10).

The Matthew 24 prophecy that Jesus gave has a timing farther in the future than the destruction of the second temple in 70 A.D. (Matthew 24:2). The first verse was related to the temple but in verse three the Disciples asked two questions: when shall this be and what shall be the sign of the return of Jesus?

Matthew 24:4-13 are discussing the signs of His coming. It mentions events related to the sorrows such as wars rumors of wars, pestilence, and famines. The love of God and Christ waxing cold and the phrase "he that endures until the end", are comments that just doesn't fit for Jesus to be speaking of Israel.

The four horses in Revelation chapter six have not fully begun to ride. We will begin to see glimpses of their effect better in the next few years; then it will be easier to determine their full release upon the earth.

When the horses do begin to ride there will be an overlapping of each of their individual effects with each other as shown in the table.

As Matthew 24:8 says, "all these things are the beginning of sorrows." Which relates to Matthew 24:6-7 and the opening of the seals in Revelation 6:1-8. The sorrows are the tribulation for the Body of Christ.

Matthew 24 Comments Related Scriptures

24:6-7	Wars and rumors of wars; nation against nation; famines, pestilences, and earthquakes	Revelation 6:1-8
24:9	Killing and hating of Believers of Christ	Revelation 6:9-11
24:10-11	Offence, betrayal, false prophets, deceiving many	Matthew 24:5; Second Thessalonians 2:3
24:12	Iniquity abounds	Second Thessalonians 2:7 (gathered to Christ)
24:14	Gospel preached to the world	Revelation 14:6; this is presenting the gospel mid-way through the tribulation
24:15	Abomination of desolation	Second Thessalonians 2:4; Revelation 13:6-7
24:16-21	Israel persecuted	Revelation 12:12-17

For yourselves know perfectly that the day of the Lord so cometh as a thief in the night.

For when they shall say, Peace and safety; then sudden destruction cometh upon them, as travail upon a women with child; and they shall not escape.

But ye, brethren, are not in darkness, that day should overtake you as a thief.

But let us, who are of the day, be sober, putting on the breastplate of faith and love; and for an helmet, the hope of salvation.

For God hath not appointed us to wrath, but to obtain salvation by our Lord Jesus Christ.

(1 Thessalonians 5:2-4;8-9)

No one knows the day or the hour of Jesus's return (Matthew 24:36), but we can know the signs and what time of the year when He comes for the Body of Christ.

When things seem tough cover your heart with faith and love; and protect your mind with the hope of salvation protecting your souls.

Since God has not appointed the Disciples of Christ to wrath (1 Thessalonians 5:9); what is the timing for the Body of Christ to be caught up?

The prophetic fulfillments relating to Jesus and the Israeli people has followed the Jewish feasts (Passover, Unleavened Bread, First Fruits, Pentecost, Trumpets, Day of Atonement, and Tabernacles).

Jesus's death (Passover), burial (Unleavened Bread), and resurrection (First Fruits) fulfilled the first three feasts.

Pentecost was fulfilled when the Holy Spirit was given in Acts chapter two. Pentecost occurs 50 days after Passover.

I always felt if we followed the feast system Christ would have to return to catch away His Bride at the start of the feast of Trumpets. Revelations 7:14-15 aligns with this as the bride is at the throne of God.

The blowing of the trumpets was the signal for the Israeli people to prepare for atonement by bringing sacrifices and offerings for repentance. Revelation 8:6 starts the sounding of the trumpets signaling the beginning of the time to repent.

The day of atonement was for the people of Israel obtaining atonement from God after trumpets because the penalty for their sin was paid. The seven-year tribulation starts in Revelation 11:1-2 just before the seventh angel sounds in Revelation 11:15. This is the 70th week spoken of in Daniel 9:24. Setting the way for Revelation 14:16 the atonement for the people of Israel.

Tabernacles signified when Israel left Egypt they dwelt in tents and God dwelt with them. I believe this is the 1000-year reign of Christ (Revelation 20:4).

The documents of the Dead Sea Scrolls point to two other feasts that are not being conducted and may give more light as to the return of Christ for His Bride. These feasts (New Wine and New Oil) were 50 days apart just as Pentecost was 50 days from Passover.

Let's see how the dates of the feast would line up in 2022 (adjusted for Sunday start dates):

Passover (first fruits the resurrection) - April 17th

Pentecost (feast of weeks) – June 5th

New Wine (grape harvest) – July 24th

New Oil (oil harvest) – September 11th

Trumpets (Rosh Hashanah) – September 25th

Atonement (Yom Kippur) – October 4th

Tabernacle (Sukkoth) – October 9th

The feast of New Wine and New Oil could be linked to the Body of Christ. Jesus used the traditions related to marriage to help define the importance of wine and oil.

When Jesus was questioned by the disciples of John asking why His disciples do not fast, He responded:

> *Can the children of the bridechamber mourn, as long as the bridegroom is with them? But the days will come, when the bridegroom shall be taken from them, and then shall they fast.*
>
> *No man putteth a piece of new cloth unto an old garment, for that which is put in to fill it up taketh from the garment, and the rent is made worse.*
>
> *Neither do men put new wine into old bottles: else the bottles break, and the wine runneth out, and the bottles perish: but they put new wine into new bottles, and both are preserved.*
>
> (Matthew 9:14-17

Our bridegroom (Christ) is taken away until He returns. The winepress treading of the grapes to produce the wine continues until He returns for it to be put in new bottles. We are left to help produce fruit of the vine (offering salvation to mankind) until the day of our gathering together unto Christ. He said in John15:5, "I am the vine and ye are the branches." The branches are the tender sprouts that appear on the vine to produce fruit (grapes for wine).

Abide in me, and I in you. As the branch cannot bear fruit of itself, except it abide in the vine; no more can ye, except ye abide in me.

(John 15:4)

The feast of New Wine is about the work of shearing salvation and the joy that comes with it.

In a parable the kingdom of heaven when 10 virgins went to meet the bridegroom; Jesus said:

And five of them were wise, and five were foolish.

They that were foolish took their lamps, and took no oil with them.

But the wise took oil in their vessels with their lamps.

While the bridegroom tarried, they all slumbered and slept.

And at midnight there was a cry made, Behold, the bridegroom cometh; go ye out to meet him.

(Matthew 25:2-6)

Oil has been used for the purpose of anointing and as a symbol of the Holy Spirit. Remember I discussed the candlesticks relating to the church in Message #4 (Revelation 1:20).

The five wise virgins took oil (the Holy Spirit) to light their way as the bridegroom approached. The five foolish had none and was not able to meet Him.

It is clear in these scriptures Jesus is speaking about us being ready when He comes.

The process of treading to remove undesirable elements from our lives (feast of New Wine); that the Holy Ghost can fill us and anoint us for service readying us to meet the bridegroom (feast of New Oil). These two new feasts clarify for me the timing of the catching away and its preparation as related to the feast of Trumpets.

Therefore, the end of Revelation 6:6, "see thou hurt[40] not the oil and the wine" is speaking about the work the Body of Christ performs through the Holy Spirt to offer salvation.

The Greek meaning of the word hurt is to be unjust toward, to wrong socially, or unjustly acts toward persons. These examples of the meaning of hurt cannot be related to sparing the fruit that produce oil and wine from the famine.

In the list of the feasts, you see the New Oil feast happens before the Feast of Trumpets this allowing the bride of Christ to be with the Lord prior to the Israeli nation experiencing the sounding of the trumpets to prepare for atonement.

The person seeking to be in the secret place of the LORD will abide under the shadow of the Almighty.

> *I will say of the LORD, He is my refuge and my fortress: my God; in him will I trust.*
>
> *Surely he shall deliver thee from the snare of the fowler, and from the noisome pestilence.*
>
> *He shall cover thee with his feathers, and under his wings shalt thou trust: his truth shall be thy shield and buckler.*
>
> *Thou shalt not be afraid for the terror by night; nor for the arrow that flieth by day;*
>
> *Nor for the pestilence that walketh in darkness; nor for the destruction that wasteth at noonday.*

A thousand shall fall at thy side, and ten thousand at thy right hand; but it shall not come nigh thee.

Only with thine eyes shalt thou behold and see the reward of the wicked.

Because thou hast made the LORD, which is my refuge, even the most High, thy habitation;

There shall no evil befall thee, neither shall any plague come nigh thy dwelling.

For he shall give his angels charge over thee, to keep thee in all thy ways.

(Psalms 91:2-11)

We will be covered by His feathers; while under His wings we can trust that His truth shall be our shield and buckler at the time of the end before we are caught up to meet Him in the air.

Prepare for the day of the Lord!

Are you ready for the end time experience?

KEY THOUGHTS PAGE

MESSAGE #8
(New Birth and New Beginning)

Harvest

This message is not about the return of Christ. It is about helping as many as possible make the decision for Christ prior to us being caught up to meet Him.

The life of Christ has always been about bringing in the harvest. Saving people from the judgement.

In Luke 10:1-3 the Lord Jesus appointed 70 to be sent out as laborers into the harvest. He gives them instructions as to how to conduct themselves while on the harvest trip as He (Jesus) pronounces woes to the places they visit for not giving heed to the laborers.

In verse 17 the laborers return with the testimony of their success people healed and even the devils were subject to them.

Then Jesus said:

I beheld satan as lightning fall from heaven.

Behold, I give unto you power to tread on serpents and scorpions, and over all the power of the enemy: and nothing shall by any means hurt you.

Notwithstanding in this rejoice not, that the spirits are subject unto you; but rather rejoice, because your names are written in heaven.

(Luke 10:18-22)

Our purpose is the same as the 70 Jesus sent out at the appointed time.

Chapter 13 of Matthew give us several parables about the kingdom of heaven.

Some of the topics in the parables are:

- Some will struggle to accept the Word of God
- There is a mixture of people in the world; those who are of Christ and those who are not
- God's kingdom is worth a great price; do all you can to enter in
- In the end there will be a sorting out of the false and the true

Our focus should be:

Go ye therefore, and teach all nations, baptizing them in the name of the Father, and of the Son, and of the Holy Ghost:

Teaching them to observe all things whatsoever I have commanded you: and, lo, I am with you alway, even unto the end of the world. Amen.

(Matthew 28:19-20)

The gentiles have been given almost 2000 years (two days) to accept Christ. I believe this is illustrated when Jesus ministered to the Samaritan woman at the well (John 4:7-30). He then stayed for two days (John 4:40) to minister to all who would come that they may know that He was the Christ.

The Samaritans believed in the tabernacle worship system that's why in Ezra 4:3 they wanted to help build the temple, but they were refuse not being descendants of Israel.

The time of the gentiles is coming to an end (the sixth day) and then we shall live in His presence. Jesus said, "all who labor and are heavy ladened let him come and I will give him rest" (Matthew 11:28).

We are traveling a journey to the promise of eternal life when death is no more; just as Israel traveled their journey in the Old Testament to the promise land. The LORD is giving all a chance to repent.

> Knowing this first, that there shall come in the last days scoffers, walking after their own lusts,
>
> And saying, Where is the promise of his coming? for since the fathers fell asleep, all things continue as they were from the beginning of the creation.
>
> (2 Peter 3:3-4)

The LORD is patient to let things play out ensuring there is no doubt as to who belongs to Him. Not that He doesn't know. It's all about us knowing who we are; whether of God or under the influence of another.

Therefore, people will begin to mock the children of God as things get worse; making it seem they were wrong about the return of Christ.

> But the heavens and the earth, which are now, by the same word are kept in store, reserved unto

fire against the day of judgment and perdition of ungodly men.

But, beloved, be not ignorant of this one thing, that one day is with the Lord as a thousand years, and a thousand years as one day.

The Lord is not slack concerning his promise, as some men count slackness; but is longsuffering to us-ward, not willing that any should perish, but that all should come to repentance.

(2 Peter 3:7-9)

Remember the parable of the 10 virgins (Matthew 25:1-10) that illustrates a warning to be ready when Jesus comes.

Be in a constant process of rejuvenation by the Holy Ghost "to hear what the Spirit is saying to His people." This was mentioned seven times in Revelation chapters two and three to each of the churches.

Listen to what is said by James:

Be patient therefore, brethren, unto the coming of the Lord. Behold, the husbandman waiteth for the precious fruit of the earth, and hath long patience for it, until he receives the early and latter rain.

Be ye also patient; stablish your hearts: for the coming of the Lord draweth nigh.

Grudge not one against another, brethren, lest ye be condemned: behold, the judge standeth before the door.

(James 5:7-9)

The life we have been given is all about helping others accept Christ through the effort of people like you and me. It may not be witnessing or preaching. It's about your life; does your life display His attributes and are you ready to explain why you believe if the opportunity comes to share it.

When the last piece of precious fruit is on board (last person to receive Christ) then shall the end come. Those who will be reaped (caught up) from the earth will have a new beginning in heaven with Christ.

Are you ready to do your part to increase the population of the Kingdom of God?

KEY THOUGHTS PAGE

MESSAGE #9

(Eternal Inspiration)

Shadows of Enlightenment

What is your validation as a Believer for the justification of your position in Christ? The shadows and ensamples (patterns) of the past reveal and solidifies our position in God based on Jesus fulfilling the law.

The New Testament is a testimony validating what God said in the Old Testament by documenting the fulfillment of prophecies related to Christ and the end time.

> *Surely he hath borne our griefs, and carried our sorrows; yet we did esteem him stricken, smitten of God, and afflicted.*
>
> *But he was wounded for our transgressions, he was bruised for our iniquities: the chastisement of our peace was upon him; and with his stripes we are healed.*

All we like sheep have gone astray; we have turned every one to his own way; and the LORD hath laid on him the iniquity of us all.

(Isaiah 53:4-6)

Jesus fulfilled the penalty of the law against us!

Think not that I am come to destroy the law, or the prophets: I am not come to destroy, but to fulfill.

For verily I say unto you, Till heaven and earth pass, one jot or one tittle shall in no wise pass from the law, till all be fulfilled.

(Matthew 5:17-18)

Jesus lets us know in these verses that the Old Testament gives us the picture (prophecy) of His earthly ministry providing the reconciliation from the law, sin, and death. He came to provide the way for us to walk in the capability of God.

For what the law could not do, in that it was weak through the flesh, God sending his own Son in the likeness of sinful flesh, and for sin, condemned sin in the flesh:

That the righteousness of the law might be fulfilled in us, who walk not after the flesh, but after the Spirit.

(Romans 8:3-4)

If we walk in the Spirit according to the Word of God, righteousness will be fulfilled in us.

The shadows of the past links the examples of the tabernacle worship and the exit from Egypt for the Israeli people and the Disciples of today through Christ Jesus.

Verse one of Hebrews chapter eight says it best, "Now of the things which we have spoken this is the sum."

Who serve unto the example and shadow of heavenly things, as Moses was admonished of God when he was about to make the tabernacle: for, See, saith he, that thou make all things according to the pattern shewed to thee in the mount.

But now hath he obtained a more excellent ministry, by how much also he is the mediator of a better covenant, which was established upon better promises.

For if that first covenant had been faultless, then should no place have been sought for the second.

For finding fault with them, he saith, Behold, the days come, saith the Lord, when I will make a new covenant with the house of Israel and with the house of Judah:

Not according to the covenant that I made with their fathers in the day when I took them by the hand to lead them out of the land of Egypt; because they continued not in my covenant, and I regarded them not, saith the Lord.

For this is the covenant that I will make with the house of Israel after those days, saith the Lord; I will put my laws into their mind, and write them in their hearts: and I will be to them a God, and they shall be to me a people:

(Hebrews 8:5-10)

The book of Hebrews was written to the Israeli community. Therefore, the above scripture is speaking to that community to help bring them to the acceptance of Jesus being their Messiah and the need for the second covenant because of their failure in the first covenant. Jesus is also the deliverer for those of us who are gentiles if we accept Him as savior.

To follow the law Moses, animal sacrifices for sin had to be made for the people, and the priest sprinkled the blood of the animals on the tabernacle, the holy place, and on all the vessels of the ministry.

> But Christ being come an high priest of good things to come, by a greater and more perfect tabernacle, not made with hands, that is to say, not of this building;
>
> (Hebrews 9:11)

The earthly tabernacle was set from the heavenly pattern of things that are in heaven. Jesus entered heaven itself; the holy place not made with hands to appear in the presence of God for us. To put away sin by His own sacrifice (Hebrews 9:14-26).

The tabernacle was a pattern and example of something very real in heaven. The LORD gave us a picture of the reality of worship and communion with Him through the tabernacle relating to the sacrifice for sin and the shekinah glory of God shining down into the Holy of Holies.

This is the perfect picture of the day of Pentecost (Acts chapter two) when the Holy Ghost came down and filled all those who were present, putting God's laws in their mind and writing them in their hearts.

But ye are a chosen generation, a royal priesthood,
an holy nation, a peculiar people; that ye should
shew forth the praises of him who hath called you
out of darkness into his marvellous light:

(1 Peter 2:9)

We now serve as priest in the heavenly tabernacle replacing the earthly example of the tabernacle in the wilderness! The shadow of things to come taking us a step closer to the reign of Christ for a thousand years on earth (Revelation 20:6); moving toward that great day when there is a new heaven and a new earth as the new Jerusalem descends from heaven (Revelation 21:1-2).

Now all these things happened unto them for
ensamples: and they are written for our admonition,
upon whom the ends of the world are come.

(1 Corinthians 10:11)

The verses before this verse detail the wilderness experience for the people of Israel. It lists the failures towards God to warn us not to do the same. The word ensamples[41] represents *a model for imitation* in this instance for a warning that the people of today would not miss out on the promise of an exciting spirit filled life which includes our promise of eternal life.

These ensamples are written for our admonition, upon whom the ends of the world are come. We should learn from their experience so that in these last days we do not repeat the same pattern of disobedience and unbelief (Hebrew 4:11).

Which are a shadow of things to come; but the body
is of Christ.

(Colossians 2:17)

The many verses before this verse details the many ordinances relating to eating, holidays, and sabbaths that showed the patterns of Old Testament worship. These ceremonies under the law were blotted out when Jesus was nailed to the cross (Colossians 2:14).

The word body[42] in this verse is the Greek word soma meaning a sound whole as the instrument of life. Christ Jesus is the sum of all interaction, ordinances, and worship toward God. The instrument of life for the world. Through acceptance of Jesus, the ordinances that showed the patterns of worship were eliminated and the world entered the time of engrafting for the gentiles to become a part of the Body of Christ.

These scriptures (*Colossians 2:17 and 1 Corinthians 10:11*) give us a real indication of how the Old Testament had a clear intent to use specific events for the purpose of revealing to the Disciples of Christ that worship toward God would go beyond the keeping of ordinances and encourage us not to fail during our journey.

> *As newborn babes, desire the sincere milk of the word, that ye may grow thereby:*
>
> *If so be ye have tasted the Lord is gracious.*
>
> *To whom coming, as unto a living stone, disallowed indeed of men, but chosen of God, and precious,*
>
> *Ye also, as lively stones, are built up a spiritual house, an holy priesthood, to offer up spiritual sacrifices, acceptable to God by Jesus Christ.*
>
> *Wherefore also it is contained in the scripture, Behold, I lay in Sion a chief corner stone, elect, precious: and he that believeth on him shall not be confounded.*
>
> *(1 Peter 2:2-6)*

The light shown by Christ illuminated the path to worship, the worship of God in Spirit and in truth! The word spiritual[43] comes from the word spirit. It was created after the day of Pentecost meaning "invisibility of power."

We are to offer up sacrifices that are endowed with the invisibility of the power of God.

Sacrifices (praying, fasting) fulfilling the call to release the bands of wickedness, to undo heavy burdens, which lets the oppressed go free, and breaks every yoke (Isaiah 58:6).

We will not be put to shame (confounded) in our efforts to demonstrate the will of God through Christ Jesus operating in our lives.

His will as stated in the example of prayer:

Thy kingdom come, Thy will be done in earth, as it is in heaven (Matthew 6:10); His will is to bring glimpses of heaven to earth.

Worship is an internal condition of the heart that allows us to enter God's presence and allows the presence of the Holy Ghost to minister to and direct us.

The opportunity for Israel to enter covenant with Christ is still open and will be fulfilled when Jesus returns during the tribulation.

> *And to make all men see what is the fellowship of the mystery, which from the beginning of the world hath been hid in God, who created all things by Jesus Christ:*
>
> *To the intent that now unto the principalities and powers in the heavenly places might be known by the church the manifold wisdom of God,*

According to the eternal purpose which he purposed in Christ Jesus our Lord:

In whom we have boldness and access with confidence by the faith of him.

(Ephesians 3:9-12)

The mystery of Jesus Christ now has given us access to the power of God through the illumination of Christ in our lives.

KEY THOUGHTS PAGE

EPILOGUE

We are entering a period of preparation for the end. My hope is that many of us walk through this period as "Women and Men of Wonder"; being directed by the Holy Spirit guiding us in His paths.

This book is to confirm a legal event that has been performed and to testify of how the testimony of Jesus Christ works in prophecy to edify God's people. To provide life experience that fulfills our documented record in heaven, being affirmed through our lives.

In October of 2020 as I read from the book of Zechariah the Spirit of the LORD reminded me of the coming events I mentioned in this work for the Body of Christ.

As His Spirit fell on me, I began to cry out for mercy; telling the Father that the people don't know and don't understand the seriousness of the current events taking place.

The Spirit reminded me of the meaning of the two olive branches (Zechariah 4:3). These are the two witnesses that are sent from the throne of God at the beginning of the last seven years (Revelation 11:3-4).

This experience let me know that the day of the Lord is fast approaching!

I always go back to the prior chapter to set the stage for what is happening in the verses I have targeted to review.

This is how I came across the verses in Zechariah 3:8 / Isaiah 4:1-2 / Isaiah 8:18, which are catalyst in the end time for those who will survive the coming world challenges.

As the world becomes fracture and torn what does this mean for the people of God? It means we leave the Babylonian culture as we understand that we are destined for great exploits. Therefore, we must seek God with urgency to be able to move obstacles by faith.

Are the people around us able to detect we are a member of God's family? Do we bring in the harvest when opportunity presents itself? Communicating the end time events that people may escape and those who may be left behind will recognize what the events mean as they come to pass.

Know this one thing, "Jesus will come again!" Will you be ready?

BIBLIOGRAPHY

Holman Bible Publishing, Giant Print Reference Bible (King James Version), Nashville, Tennessee, 1996.

James Strong, LLD, STD, "The New Strong's Expanded Exhaustive Concordance" of the Bible (Red Letter Edition), Nashville, TN: Thomas Nelson Publishers, 2010

ABOUT THE AUTHOR

Enoch Elijah has a Master of Arts degree in biblical studies. Elijah has self-publish two other works "Insights for Believers" and "God Is". Has served the church as Men's Sunday Bible School Leader, Men's Group Leader, and Youth Sunday School Leader. He has been invited to minister for congregations in Oklahoma, Texas, Missouri, and Louisiana.

Thy kingdom come; Thy will be done in earth, as it is in heaven.

(Matthew 6:10)

APPENDIX

All scripture references were taken from The Holy Bible: King James Version, Holman Bible Publishing, Nashville, Tennessee, 1996.

DEADICATION
2 Timothy 3:1

EPIGRAPH
Numbers 6:24-26

PREFACE

INTRODUCTION
Revelation 17:3; 17:5; **Zechariah** 1:3; 1:14-15; 1:20-21; **Ephesians** 2:10; **James** 1:21-22; **Haggai** 1:13

WEAKENED BELIEFS
Revelation 18:2-4; **1 Timothy** 1:9-10; **Matthew** 24:10; **Proverbs** 13:24; **Isaiah** 5:20-23; **2 Timothy** 3:2-3; **Matthew** 13:27-29

LEAVE BABYLON
1 Kings 18:21; **Zechariah** 2:7; 4:6; 4:3; **Revelation** 11:4; **Zechariah** 4:10; 4:9; **Revelation** 5:6; 1:1-3; **1 Peter** 4:17; **2 Peter** 1:3-4; **Matthew** 7:13

SEEK TO HEAR

Matthew 13:3-9; John 1:4-5; 1:14; Hebrews 4:12; Psalms 1:1-3; John 5:39; Matthew 7:8; Romans 12:2; Philippians 2:5; Romans 7:22-23; 5:5; 15:13; Psalms 18:1-2; John 1:16; Philippians 4:11; James 2:18; 1 Thessalonians 2:12; 1 Corinthians 4:20; John 16:23-25; Matthew 27:50-51; 2 Corinthians 6:16; Mark 16:17-18; 1 Corinthians 2:4-5; Ephesians 3:17-18; Revelation 3:12

CHILDREN OF GOD

Romans 8:7; John 13:34-35; Luke 11:52; Zechariah 4:2; Revelation 1:20; Ephesians 2:5-7; 1:17-20; Romans 8:14-17; John 5:20-22; 14:12-13; Galatians 4:3-7

PEOPLE OF WONDER

Zechariah 3:8; Isaiah 8:18; 8:19-20; 2 Corinthians 11:14-15; Ephesians 6:12; John 15:13-15; 14:12-18; 2 Kings 6:15-17; Psalms 91:11; Hebrews 1:7; 1:14

MOUNTAIN MOVERS

Philippians 3:8; 1:10-11; 2 Peter 1:3-4; 1:11; Zechariah 4:7; Mark 11:23-24; John 15:5-6; Hebrews 11:1-3; Mark 9:23-24; 1 Peter 2:5; Hebrews 13:15; Romans 4:17; John 12:35-36; Ezekiel 22:30; Habakkuk 2:1-4; John 17:15-20; Ephesians 3:10

END TIMES

1 Thessalonians 4:16-17; 2 Thessalonians 2:1-8; Matthew 7:19-23; 2 Timothy 3:5; James 2:19-20; 1 Peter 4:17-19; Luke 21:17-19; 1 Thessalonians 5:2-4; 5:8-9; Matthew 9:14-17; John 15:4; Matthew 25:2-6; Psalms 91:2-11

HARVEST

Luke 10:18-22; Matthew 28:19-20; 2 Peter 3:3-4; 3:7-9; James 5:7-9

SHADOWS OF ENLIGHTENMENT
Isaiah 53:4-6; **Matthew** 5:17-18; **Romans** 8:3-4; **Hebrews** 8:5-10; 9:11; **1 Peter** 2:9; **1 Corinthians** 10:11; **Colossians** 2:17; **1 Peter** 2:2-6; **Ephesians** 3:9-12

EPILOGUE

ENDNOTES

All word references and meanings are taken from the

James Strong, LLD, STD, The New Strong's Expanded Exhaustive Concordance of the Bible (Red Letter Edition), Nashville, TN: Thomas Nelson Publishers, 2010.

Old Testament word meanings are taken from the Hebrew and Aramaic Dictionary (p. 1 through p. 303) and New Testament word meanings are taken from the Greek Dictionary (p. 1 through p. 277) in the back section of The New Strong's Expanded Exhaustive Concordance of the Bible.

1   **Fray** – Hebrew Strong's number 2729
2   **Menstealers** - Greek Strong's number 405
3   **Commandments** - Greek Strong's number 1785
4   **Blasphemers** – Greek Strong's number 987
5   **Tares** – Greek Strong's number 2215
6   **Swear** – Hebrew Strong's number 7650
7   **Young** – Hebrew Strong's number 970
8   **Deliver** - Hebrew Strong's number 4422
9   **Zerubbabel** - Hebrew Strong's number 2216
10 **Patience** - Greek Strong's number 5281
11 **Temptation** - Greek Strong's number 3986
12 **Hear** - Greek Strong's number 191
13 **El** – Hebrew Strong's number 410

14 **Shadday** – Hebrew Strong's number 7706

15 **Jehovah** – Hebrew Strong's number 3068

16 **Adon** – Hebrew Strong's number 113

17 **Adonay** – Hebrew Strong's number 136

18 **Mind** - Greek Strong's number 3563

19 **Mind** - Greek Strong's number 5426

20 **Members** - Greek Strong's number 3196

21 **Patient** - Greek Strong's number 5281

22 **Abba** - Greek Strong's number 5

23 **Fellows** – Hebrew Strong's number 7453

24 **Wondered** – Hebrew Strong's number 4159

25 **Joshua** – Hebrew Strong's number 3091

26 **Jesus** - Greek Strong's number 2424

27 **Tsaba** – Hebrew Strong's number 6635

28 **Ministers** - Greek Strong's number 3011

29 **Fire** - Greek Strong's number 4442

30 **Kingdom** - Greek Strong's number 932

31 **Faith** – Greek Strong's number 4102

32 **Beautiful** – Greek Strong's number 5611

33 **Withholdeth** – Greek Strong's number 2722

34 **Taken** – Greek Strong's number 1096

35 **Mystery**   Greek Strong's number 3466

36 **Iniquity** – Greek Strong's number 458

37 **Godliness** – Greek Strong's number 2150

38 **Possess** – Greek Strong's number 2932

39 **Souls** – Greek Strong's number 5590

40 **Hurt** – Greek Strong's number 91

41 **Ensamples** – Greek Strong's number 5179

42 **Body** - Greek Strong's number 4983

43 **Spiritual** - Greek Strong's number 4152

Printed in the United States
by Baker & Taylor Publisher Services